Muhammad Ali

by
Arthur Diamond

Lucent Books, P.O. Box 289011, San Diego, CA 92198-9011

These and other titles are included in The Importance Of biography series:

Alexander the Great	Galileo Galilei	Sir Isaac Newton
Muhammad Ali	Martha Graham	Richard M. Nixon
Louis Armstrong	Stephen Hawking	Louis Pasteur
Napoleon Bonaparte	Jim Henson	Jackie Robinson
Rachel Carson	Harry Houdini	Anwar Sadat
Cleopatra	Thomas Jefferson	Margaret Sanger
Christopher Columbus	Chief Joseph	John Steinbeck
Marie Curie	Malcolm X	Jim Thorpe
Thomas Edison	Margaret Mead	Mark Twain
Albert Einstein	Michelangelo	H.G. Wells
Benjamin Franklin	Wolfgang Amadeus Mozart	

Dedication

For my cousin, Leslie Diamond

Acknowledgments

The author wishes to express appreciation for the contributions of Gary Rubin and the late Julius Bromberg to this book.

Library of Congress Cataloging-in-Publication Data

Diamond, Arthur
    Muhammad Ali / by Arthur Diamond
       p. cm.—(The Importance of)
    Includes bibliographical references (p.) and index.
    ISBN 1-56006-060-3 (acid-free paper)
    1. Ali, Muhammad, 1942- —Juvenile literature. 2. Boxers (Sports)—United States—Biography—Juvenile literature. [1. Ali, Muhammad, 1942-   2. Boxers (Sports)] I. Title. II. Series.
GV1132.A44D53   1995
796.8'3'092—dc20   93-47623
[B]   CIP
                              AC

Contents

Foreword

THE IMPORTANCE OF biography series deals with individuals who have made a unique contribution to history. The editors of the series have deliberately chosen to cast a wide net and include people from all fields of endeavor. Individuals from politics, music, art, literature, philosophy, science, sports, and religion are all represented. In addition, the editors did not restrict the series to individuals whose accomplishments have helped change the course of history. Of necessity, this criterion would have eliminated many whose contribution was great, though limited. Charles Darwin, for example, was responsible for radically altering the scientific view of the natural history of the world. His achievements continue to impact the study of science today. Others, such as Chief Joseph of the Nez Percé, played a pivotal role in the history of their own people. While Joseph's influence does not extend much beyond the Nez Percé, his nonviolent resistance to white expansion and his continuing role in protecting his tribe and his homeland remain an inspiration to all.

These biographies are more than factual chronicles. Each volume attempts to emphasize an individual's contributions both in his or her own time and for posterity. For example, the voyages of Christopher Columbus opened the way to European colonization of the New World. Unquestionably, his encounter with the New World brought monumental changes to both Europe and the Americas in his day. Today, however, the broader impact of Columbus's voyages is being critically scrutinized. *Christopher Columbus,* as well as every biography in The Importance Of series, includes and evaluates the most recent scholarship available on each subject.

Each author includes a wide variety of primary and secondary source quotations to document and substantiate his or her work. All quotes are footnoted to show readers exactly how and where biographers derive their information, as well as to provide stepping stones to further research. These quotations enliven the text by giving readers eyewitness views of the life and times of each individual covered in The Importance Of series.

Finally, each volume is enhanced by photographs, bibliographies, chronologies, and comprehensive indexes. For both the casual reader and the student engaged in research, The Importance Of biographies will be a fascinating adventure into the lives of people who have helped shape humanity's past and present, and who will continue to shape its future.

Important Dates in the Life of Muhammad Ali

1942 — Cassius Clay is born January 17 in Louisville, Kentucky.

1942 — Fights his first televised bout on the local show *Tomorrow's Champions.*

1954

1960 — Wins the gold medal as a light heavyweight boxer at the Olympic Games in Rome. First professional fight, against Tunney Hunsaker.

1960 — Wins world championship by defeating Sonny Liston on February 25. Announces his membership in the Nation of Islam and his change of name, to Muhammad Ali.

1964 — Refuses induction into the armed forces of the United States and is stripped of title and banned from boxing.

1967 — Exiled from Nation of Islam by Elijah Muhammad for wanting to box again; several months later, after apologies and intervention by Elijah Muhammad's son, Ali is reinstated.

1969 — Returns to the ring to defeat Jerry Quarry in Atlanta on October 26.

1970

1971 — Loses first bout as professional boxer to Joe Frazier in Madison Square Garden, March 8. On June 28 the Supreme Court reverses his 1967 conviction for refusing induction to the military.

1973 — On March 31 suffers broken jaw in first round of twelve-round fight with Ken Norton, who wins by unanimous decision. Ali wins decision against Norton in rematch on September 10.

1974 — Defeats Frazier in a rematch. Defeats George Foreman in Zaire on October 30 to regain the heavyweight championship of the world.

1975 — Defeats Frazier again in the Thrilla in Manila.

1978 — Loses the title to Leon Spinks in February, then wins it back from Spinks seven months later to capture heavyweight crown an unprecedented third time.

1979 — Announces his retirement from the ring.

1980 — Loses in comeback attempt, to world champion Larry Holmes in Las Vegas.

1981 — Loses last fight of boxing career to Trevor Berbick in Nassau and announces final retirement.

1984 — Diagnosed with Parkinson's syndrome.

The Forsaken Medal

In the fall of 1960, after his return to the United States from the Rome Olympics, Cassius Clay felt on top of the world. The young light heavyweight boxer had won the gold medal after defeating Polish champion Zbigniew Pietrzykowski in the boxing finals. In the first minutes of the three-round match, the left-handed Pole had presented a problem for the lightning-quick Clay, who was accustomed to fighting right-handed opponents. But Clay found a way to adjust and was able to take control of the fight, finishing strongly and leaving no one in doubt about who was the superior boxer.

Upon his triumphant return to the United States, Clay's first stop was New York City, where he ambled through the

Cassius Clay (far right) poses for a group photo with members of the 1960 U.S. Olympic Boxing Team. In Rome, Clay defeated Polish champion Zbigniew Pietrzykowski for the Olympic gold medal.

streets in his red, white, and blue training jacket. He shook hands and exchanged jokes with all who recognized him. To those who seemed not to know who he was, he brashly announced his Olympic feats and proclaimed that he was going to become the heavyweight boxing champion of the world.

When he returned to his hometown of Louisville, Kentucky, Clay was happy to see many proud citizens turn out at the airport to welcome him. The outgoing young man responded to Louisville's admiration by writing a poem about his Olympic experience:

How Cassius Took Rome
by Cassius Clay, Jr.
To make America the greatest is my
  goal,
So I beat the Russians, and I beat the
  Poles
And for the USA won the medal of
  gold
Italians said, "You're greater than Cassius of old."
We like your name, we like your game
So make Rome your home if you will.
I said I appreciate kind hospitality
But the USA is my country still
'Cause they're waiting to welcome me
  in Louisville.[1]

At his home, Clay found that his father had painted the front steps red, white, and blue. Cassius Clay, triumphant in the Rome Olympics, basked in the hospitality of his hometown.

Not everyone offered goodwill, though. Shortly after his return to Louisville, he faced the kind of bigotry and prejudice that plagued African Americans in much of the United States. As he recalled in his autobiography, *The Greatest: My Own Story*, the trouble started when he was refused service in a Louisville restaurant that served whites only. Even the fact that he was wearing his Olympic gold medal made no impression on the restaurant owner. "I don't give a damn who he is," the owner remarked after a waitress identified the young boxer. "I don't serve niggers."[2]

Blacks Refused Service

What happened to Clay had happened to other young black people seeking service in restaurants, shopping centers, movie theaters, and drugstores throughout the South. Earlier in 1960 four young black men in downtown Greensboro, North Carolina, had demanded and were refused service at an all-white Woolworth's lunch counter. In protest they remained sitting at the counter and refused to leave. The next day other black students joined the lunch counter protest, and they in turn were joined by white students from a nearby women's college. Sit-ins, as such protests were called, had begun in the 1950s and would continue into the 1960s, as the fight for civil rights and equality gained momentum.

Feeling "shamed and shocked and lonesome,"[3] Clay left the restaurant. He and his friend Ronnie King rode off on their motorbikes—and were pursued by a gang of white toughs on huge, gleaming Harley-Davidson motorcycles. The toughs had been part of the scene at the restaurant.

They wanted Clay's Olympic medal. For it, they promised, Clay and his friend could have safe passage back to his neighborhood. Of course Clay refused, and the chase began again, only to end with Cassius

Black students in Greensboro, North Carolina stage a sit-in at a whites-only Woolworth's lunch counter after being refused service. Even an Olympic gold medal failed to protect Clay from similar discrimination.

and Ronnie trapped on the Jefferson County Bridge linking Kentucky and Indiana. Below swirled the waters of the Ohio River.

In a quick but fierce battle, Cassius and Ronnie beat up the gang leaders badly enough to send them limping back to the others with orders to disperse. The two friends watched the gang ride off. Then, leaning against the bridge railing, Cassius removed the medal from around his neck. Frowning, he studied it. Suddenly, before Ronnie could interfere, Clay let his gold medal slip through his fingers and fall down, down, into the waters of the Ohio.

In his autobiography Clay offers a moving rationale for discarding his Olympic medal. He also gives a hint of future conflicts between the expectations of others and the dictates of his conscience. He writes:

> The Olympic medal had been the most precious thing that had ever come to me. I worshiped it. It was a proof of performance, status, a symbol of belonging, of being a part of a team, a country, a world. It was my way of redeeming myself with my teachers and schoolmates at Central High, of letting them know that although I had not won scholastic victories, there was something inside me capable of victory.
>
> How could I explain to Ronnie I wanted something that meant more than that? Something that was as proud of me as I would be of it. Something that would let me be what I knew I had to be, my own kind of champion.[4]

In the years Cassius Clay spent pursuing that something—which may well have been his obedience to his own conscience—America struggled to keep up with him. Boxing fans, at first skeptical of his unusual fighting style and angry at his boasting and promotional antics, would in time acknowledge him as perhaps the greatest boxer of all time. The general public, alarmed first by his allegiance to

Clay proudly displays his gold medal to admiring Italians. Clay would come to treasure his ability to remain true to himself more highly than rewards or admiration.

the radical Nation of Islam, then enraged by his refusal to be drafted into the military, would eventually accept his right to exercise religious freedom and his decision to dissent with the government. African Americans, periodically disturbed by his early boasts and publicity stunts, ultimately accepted and embraced him as a source of pride, determination, and hope.

Gazing down from the Jefferson County Bridge, his Olympic gold medal now gone forever, young Cassius Clay had begun to realize that rewards didn't really matter to him, and that recognition for his accomplishments didn't matter much, either. He would not pursue rewards bestowed by others and, therefore, beyond his control. He would become his own kind of champion—regardless of what anybody else thought, regardless of whether his Olympic gold medal dangled from his neck or lay at the bottom of the Ohio River.

1 Cassius Clay

Cassius Marcellus Clay Jr. was born on January 17, 1942, in Louisville, Kentucky. He was the elder son of Cassius Marcellus Clay and Odessa Grady Clay. Cassius's brother Rudolph Valentino Clay was born a few years later, and the family lived in a neat house in a black working-class neighborhood in the west end of the city.

Since the Civil War, Kentucky, with Louisville as its largest city, has been influenced by its nearness to the so-called northern states. It has a history of having more liberal attitudes toward African Americans than deep-South states such as Georgia, Mississippi, and Alabama. During the Civil War Kentucky never seceded from the Union like its southernmost neighbors; it chose to remain neutral.

In many respects, though, Kentucky has not been different from other southern states. Indeed, Kentucky did not voluntarily free its slaves, and Kentucky blacks led lives filled with daily humiliations up to and including the time of World War II. Segregation was strongly in evidence. Throughout the state blacks and whites were required to drink from different water fountains, sit in different parts

Clay was born and raised in the state of Kentucky during the 1940s and 50s, where segregation laws still required blacks and whites to drink from separate fountains.

of city buses, and eat meals in different restaurants. For blacks, city services, such as sanitation and sewage, were inferior to those for whites.

Throughout its history Louisville has boasted tremendous wealth. It is here that manufacturing families like Reynolds, makers of Reynolds Wrap, and Brown-Forman, owners of one of the country's largest distilleries, made their homes and ran their businesses. Here one finds the glorious beauty of Churchill Downs, where the Kentucky Derby horse race is an annual event.

However, African Americans in Louisville have historically had little or no access to this wealth. Blacks lived separately from whites, in relative obscurity and poverty in ghettos like the notorious Snake Town and other downtown neighborhoods. Blacks knew enough to stay out of white neighborhoods, where they would certainly encounter name-calling and threats.

Family Influences

While the Clay family had few direct problems with racism, Cassius Clay Sr., also known as Cash, was a frustrated artist and singer, and he told anyone who asked that it was white society that had kept him from becoming a true artist. White society, he claimed, had suppressed him and produced a man whose real talents would never be known.

Cassius Jr.'s grandfather, Herman Clay, also held white society in contempt. Herman had worked hard for years cleaning spittoons in whites-only taverns in Louisville before he managed to start his own business selling ice and wood. When he achieved success, remembering his treatment by whites in the taverns, he refused to let any white man into his own home.

Clay's father Cash (right) was a frustrated artist and singer who would often fly into fits of rage and anger. In contrast, his mother Odessa (center) was a soft-spoken, gentle woman.

Sometimes Cash would fly into fits of anger and rage, and usually he headed to the barroom to calm down. He also sometimes beat Odessa. This is confirmed by police reports of responses to calls for help from the Clay home. Cassius Jr., however, never showed resentment for the way his father sometimes treated his mother. Some sources suggest that Cash might have tried to strike his sons, too. Dr. Ferdie Pacheco, who would one day work in the young boxer's corner, reports that Clay remarked, "Maybe that's when I learned to float like a butterfly. . . . I owe my defense to my father."[5]

Cash's wife, Odessa, was a soft-spoken, gentle, religious woman. She worked in Louisville as a household domestic. When her husband went into his rages, she was the calming voice; she would soothe him as well as comfort the children until Cash's mood passed or he left the house. Odessa was a Baptist and attended church every Sunday. She passed her belief in gentleness, forgiveness, and love to her two sons.

Cassius was always close to his younger brother, Rudolph, or Rudy. When their mother would get ready to spank Rudy, Cassius would stand in front of his younger brother, protecting him. Even as the two entered adulthood and tended to their own families and affairs, they remained close.

An Active, Precocious Child

Those closest to him insist that Cassius Clay Jr. was born to be a boxer. His father recalls that his first son "came into this world with a good body and a big head

The close, protective relationship that Clay shared with his younger brother Rudy (left) would continue into adulthood.

that was the image of Joe Louis. That made me real proud. I loved Joe Louis."[6]

Moreover, Cassius's first words as a baby were "gee-gee," and this quickly became his mother's nickname for him. Clay would later explain his first words: "I wanted to let folks know I was on my way up to the Golden Gloves."[7]

Young Cassius was a precocious child. His mother remembers that at two years old, Cassius never sat still and always walked on tiptoe. Also, Cassius was self-assured at an early age. He played with older children and became their leader. His mother remembers that he had, at age four, "all the confidence in the world."[8]

What Boxing Requires

Cassius Clay, later Muhammad Ali, made boxing look easy. Audiences marveled at the way he danced and clowned in the ring and made the effort of boxing appear effortless. In his book Black Lights: Inside the World of Professional Boxing, *Thomas Hauser talks about those who become boxers, and all the hard work they go through to survive in the profession:*

"Boxing is one of the few professions that gives people from the underclass an opportunity to earn large sums of money and be heroes in their native land. It offers a young man hope, and the possibility that he will someday possess a world title once held by a god like Joe Louis or Sugar Ray Robinson. There is a unique importance to the heroes of old because they stand for the proposition that greatness in boxing is not a mirage. But in reality most fighters never become champions. The vast majority never even advance to the status of 'main event' fighters. And along the way a price is paid—by some, for good value in return; for others, not so good. The price is high.

Being a fighter is more than a job; it's a way of life. Everything a fighter does affects his profession—what he eats, what he drinks, how he sleeps, what he does at night. Yet unless a fighter is considered a valuable 'prospect,' there's no one to push and prod him on. Thus the trade requires extraordinary self-motivation."

Throughout childhood Cassius continued to lead. While passive in the classroom, he was naturally athletic and would get his friends together in the street for games of touch football. While at times he loved to play a peaceful game of marbles, at other times he requested that his friends throw rocks at him. He wanted to see if he was quick enough to be able to get out of the way. Rudy later recalled that during the many times Cassius egged him on, he could never hit him with a rock. Cassius was simply too quick.

Being quick on his feet, though, could not keep Cassius from losing an important possession. In October 1954 twelve-year-old Cassius left a bazaar at a local gym and found that his brand new bicycle was gone. It was a Schwinn with red lights and whitewall tires—a recent gift. "I betcha we paid almost $60 for that wheel," his mother later remembered.[9]

Joe Martin

Cassius was angry and tearful. He vowed to whip whoever had made off with his bike. He went back into the gym and was told to go to the recreation center and report the crime to officer Joe Martin. Martin coached young boxers in his spare time and explained to the tearful boy that he had better learn to fight before he went out to whip anybody. Cassius, tears still in his eyes, looked around in awe at his surroundings—boys and men worked out, together and alone, skipping rope, punching the heavy bag, sparring. The air smelled of sweat and hard work.

Cassius told Martin that he was indeed interested in learning how to box. Martin gave Clay an application and told him to watch the televised matches that week. Martin's fighters were featured in a weekly show called *Tomorrow's Champions*. As writers Edna and Art Rust report, "That Saturday Cassius watched the show, filled out the application, and proclaimed, 'I want to be a boxer.'"[10]

At first Clay's parents opposed his plan. Boxing lessons were another expense in a household struggling to meet its budget. But Clay's parents seemed to understand that with all the temptations of street life, including the gangs that roamed Snake Town, and with their eldest son's lack of interest in schoolwork, boxing lessons might be a very good thing indeed. They let him join Joe Martin's gym.

A Way to Rise Up

In the 1950s athletics were one of the few recognized ways for an African American to rise to the top of a profession. In the early fifties the victories of Joe Louis, the Brown Bomber, were fresh in everyone's mind; in the previous decade, Louis had fought for American pride and had defeated German hope Max Schmeling. Fifty years before, at the turn of the century,

The naturally athletic Clay began boxing at the age of twelve. Within one year he was making appearances on Tomorrow's Champions, *a television program featuring top amateur boxers.*

the great Jack Johnson, a black man, had dominated boxing—much to the chagrin of whites across the nation, who sought—and ultimately found—a Great White Hope to defeat him.

In other sports African Americans had also drawn world attention. In the 1936 Olympics in Berlin, Jesse Owens's performances in track-and-field events did not support ideas of white racial superiority despite the best efforts of Adolf Hitler's Aryan so-called "supermen." And in 1947, when Cassius Clay was five years old,

Much to the chagrin of whites across the country, Jack Johnson became the first black heavyweight champion in 1908.

Jackie Robinson had become the first black to play professional baseball in the U.S. major leagues.

Young Clay's earliest boxing hero was Sugar Ray Robinson. Robinson was quick and skillful in the ring and flamboyant outside it. Robinson had his own entourage, or group of followers, and he always had an attractive woman on his arm. Clay was especially impressed with Robinson's publicized yearly purchase of a new Cadillac, each a different pastel color.

Clay took to boxing easily and with great enthusiasm. Despite school and church responsibilities, he routinely made the time to train, and he devoted as much time as possible to it each day. His first trainer, Joe Martin, later recalled, "He stood out because, I guess, he had more determination than most boys, and he had the speed to get him someplace."[11]

Clay was determined to get someplace quickly. He trained with Martin and also at

a gym across town run by Fred Stoner. His devotion to training soon paid off: In 1954 Martin picked him to appear on the local television show *Tomorrow's Champions,* and he beat his opponent in a split decision— one in which the winner receives the vote of two out of three judges. His ability made his parents proud. His father said that the boy had a punch like Joe Louis. Cassius vowed to his mother that he would be the "champion of the world."[12]

Emmett Till

In 1955 something happened that shook up Cassius—and much of the nation. Emmett Till, a fourteen-year-old black teenager from Chicago, was brutally murdered while visiting relatives in Mississippi. Rumor said that he had looked the wrong

The quick and flamboyant Sugar Ray Robinson was Clay's earliest boxing hero.

Emmett Till's mother (seated) protests the acquittal of her son's alleged murderers with members of New York City's black community. The murder had a profound impact on young Clay.

young Cassius felt a deep affinity for the murdered boy. "I couldn't get Emmett out of my mind," he would later say.[13] Emmett Till's death made real to Cassius and to many other Americans the great problem of racism in the country.

Growing Up in the Fifties

Outside the boxing gym where young Cassius toiled, the nation struggled with civil rights. Having endured slavery until the Civil War, and condemned afterwards to wear chains of social, economic, and educational injustice, African Americans had begun to organize in an effort to change the laws that kept them segregated from white society.

Black veterans of World War II were representative of the injustice American blacks had suffered. Having risked their lives for their country—as many blacks had also done during the Civil War and World War I—black veterans came home from the battlefield to 1950s America and found the same bigotry, prejudice, and violence they had hoped to forever leave behind. They were still being treated as second-class citizens: still forced to use "colored-only" restaurants and drinking fountains, still required to sit in the back of the public buses, still constrained to send their children to inferior, segregated schools.

New laws promised equality for blacks but did not deliver. In 1954—the year Clay discovered boxing—the Supreme Court ruled on a landmark case, *Brown v. Board of Education* (of Topeka, Kansas). The Court had announced that new laws would make sure black children got the same education as white children; but in

way at a white woman in a store, and the next day he had been dragged from his relatives' house by a group of whites; the men beat Till and then drowned him. Though the FBI and witnesses supplied strong evidence against the alleged attackers, the white men were judged not guilty by local all-white juries.

In Chicago the boy was memorialized by his distraught mother. She refused to bury her son quickly. Thousands of mourners viewed his open casket and the brutalized body within. The nation followed the case closely. African-American leaders were especially outraged.

Young Cassius seemed to be struck more by this incident than anything else that happened in the world outside Louisville. He and Till were nearly the same age. Clay's father had been talking about the story—as were others in black communities all around the country—and

A Young Boaster

John Hennessey, in his book Muhammad Ali: "The Greatest," *talks about two fledgling qualities of young Cassius Clay—his willingness to train and his unwillingness to keep quiet:*

"Training came easy to Clay. Because his family was poor, there was seldom enough money for Cassius and his brother Rudy to take the bus to school each day. So Clay used to race it, pretending in part that he actually wanted to. He also used to measure up [compete] against the horses at the local racecourse when they were riding out each day. But even at that early age, despite a strict upbringing by his parents, he had become a boaster and was seen by some as an obnoxious big mouth. His trainer, Joe Martin, even threatened to pull him out of the Olympic trials at the semi-final stage if he didn't stop bragging following local newspaper criticism."

reality the new laws were ignored. In the South, Jim Crow statutes continued to enforce racial segregation. (*Jim Crow* was the term used for a system of laws and customs in the South that segregated blacks from white society; the name came from a minstrel song.) In the North blacks continued to face job, housing, and school discrimination.

In 1955, in addition to the Till murder, another event related to racism and civil rights drew national attention. In December of that year Rosa Parks, a seamstress in Montgomery, Alabama, defied the Jim Crow city bus laws and refused to move to the back of the bus. She was fined for breaking the law. This led to a citywide boycott by Montgomery's blacks of the city buses, a boycott organized by a young preacher named Martin Luther King Jr. The boycott lasted more than a year and ended with a favorable Supreme Court ruling and the desegregation of public buses.

In Training

While the fight for civil rights gained momentum, Cassius Clay worked at becoming the best boxer he could be. Soon after being introduced to boxing at age twelve, Cassius made training a priority in his life; by his high school years it had become his passion. He got up every morning and ran as many as six miles in a local park before going to school. His school performance was mediocre—he often slept through classes. He ran again at lunchtime, and after school he worked at a part-time job for local Nazareth College. After work he went to Martin's gym for a two-hour workout. His persistence and discipline were impressive. "It was impossible to discourage him," Joe Martin later remembered. "He was easily the hardest worker of any kid I ever taught, and I've taught hundreds in my time."[14]

Montgomery blacks boycotted city buses and demanded an end to segregation after Rosa Parks (right) refused to move to the back of a bus and was fined for violating Montgomery's Jim Crow bus laws.

Not only did Clay train his body for boxing, but he also educated his mind for boxing. He pumped anyone and everyone for any kind of helpful information about the art of fighting. He also experimented with boxing styles. One style he adopted involved an unorthodox, sudden backward lean to avoid an oncoming punch to the face. Other boxers and trainers criticized this tactic and urged him to stick with the standard side-to-side way of "slipping" a punch. But to Cassius it felt right. He knew, too, from his research into boxing history, that Jack Johnson had used the same leaning technique.

Clay was an ardent student of boxing and a diligent trainer, but perhaps more than anything else, Cassius Clay had confidence. This was evident from the very beginning, and it never failed to impress others. Fighting as an amateur, he promot-

ed his upcoming bouts—which he typically won—by ringing doorbells in Louisville and advising people to come down to Martin's gym or to watch the television so they would not miss seeing the future heavyweight champion of the world in action.

The White Cassius Clay

At some point during high school, the young boxer discovered the identity of the man he was named after. Cassius Marcellus Clay, a white man, had been a prominent statesman in the nineteenth century. He had been an abolitionist—one who supported the end of slavery—and had freed his own slaves in support of that view. He had also been a friend of President Abraham Lincoln, and in the 1860s he was the U.S. ambassador to Russia.

Clay was angered to discover that although the nineteenth-century statesman Cassius Marcellus Clay (pictured) fought for the abolition of slavery, he did not believe in racial equality.

But Clay learned another important—and distressing—thing about the man he was named after. Cassius Marcellus Clay, while having freed his slaves, thought of them as members of an inferior race. The following passage appeared in one of the books that Cassius had searched through: "I am of the opinion that the Caucasian or white is the superior race; they have a larger and better formed brain; much more developed form and exquisite structure."[15]

This discovery did not sit well with the young black boxer. "This is the name I'm supposed to be proud of?" he asked himself.[16] Later he would change this offending name.

Clay had a brilliant amateur career, appearing in 108 fights and losing only 8 during the years 1954-1960. He won several Golden Gloves titles in Kentucky, and in 1960 he won the national Golden Gloves heavyweight title in New York City. In that year he also won the Amateur Athletic Union (AAU) championship.

Clay's next goal was to become an Olympic champion in the 1960 games to be held in Rome, Italy. He worked hard and won a spot on the Olympic boxing team, and he was excited about prevailing in Rome against the best amateurs in the world.

He was not excited about actually getting to Rome, though. He feared flying. At first Clay adamantly refused to fly. He wanted to get to Rome some other way—by boat, perhaps. But his trainer, Joe Martin, had a talk with the young boxer. Martin explained that Clay could indeed take a boat, but the trip would take him two weeks and by then the Olympics would be over. Martin explained that if Clay wanted to be heavyweight champion of the world, he would have to fly to Rome and box in the Olympics—it was as simple as that. Clay understood and agreed to fly.

The Olympics

In Rome's Villaggio Olimpico—the Olympic Village—Cassius Clay was probably the most popular athlete in residence. He spent much time meeting other athletes, shaking their hands, being friendly—and telling them how he was going to be champion of the world. Says sports columnist Arthur Daly, "He was winning friends and influencing people everywhere."[17] A teammate of Clay's said, "You would have thought he was running for mayor."[18]

The eighteen-year-old set about winning the championship. He won his first three fights without problems, but in the

Clay trains for the 1960 Golden Gloves title with fellow boxer Jimmy Ellis (left).

Clay poses with fellow Olympic gold-medal winners upon their return to the United States. Clay's love for the United States earned him the image of the "All-American Boy."

final bout, for the gold medal, he faced Zbigniew Pietrzykowski, the Polish champion—a southpaw (left-hander). Clay had trouble with the other fighter at first, but by the end of the fight he was pounding away with sharp combination punches that stunned the Pole and impressed the judges, who awarded Clay the decision.

Moreover, his press image was that of the All-American Boy. This came through strongly when, in a televised press conference, a Soviet reporter asked an uncomfortable question. The reporter wanted to know how gold-medalist Clay felt about not being able to eat with white people when he got back to the United States. "Tell your readers," Clay shot back proudly, "that we got qualified people working on that problem, and I'm not worried about the outcome. To me, the USA is still the best country in the world, counting yours."[19]

After winning the gold medal, Clay refused to take it off. "I didn't take that medal off for forty-eight hours," he later recalled. "I even wore it to bed. I didn't sleep too good because I had to sleep on my back so that the medal wouldn't cut me. But I didn't care, I was the Olympic champion."[20]

2 "Who Made Me—Is Me!"

Back in Louisville after the Olympics, Cassius Clay focused on lining up fights for himself. With the help of his father, the eighteen-year-old served as his own promoter and trainer for his first professional fight. On October 29, 1960, in Louisville, Clay faced West Virginian Tunney Hunsaker, an older, full-time police chief and part-time boxer. Clay handily won a six-round decision over the more experienced but less talented fighter.

Still, Clay knew that talent alone was not guaranteed to get him what he wanted—the world championship. He knew he needed professional management, and he sought it first from Sugar Ray Robinson, his boyhood boxing idol. But Robinson, nearing the end of his career, declared himself too busy and shooed the young man away. Joe Louis, another Clay hero, was also unavailable. Offers to manage Clay came from around the world, but few were worth considering. Cassius Clay Sr. was especially careful and wanted to make sure his son got the best possible deal, one that would protect him and assure that he would earn as much as possible.

Cash Clay had good reason to be careful about who would manage his son. Boxing was, in effect, an outlaw sport. It had never had a national commissioner, welfare and pension programs, or uniform

medical and safety standards. With no central, legal organizing body to run it, boxing had, in fact, been run by outlaws. Author Robert Lipsyte maintains that gangsters entered boxing because legitimate businessmen did not want to risk their money or reputations on the sport. "Not only did [the racketeers] have unaccounted cash to spend and no reputations

Following his Olympic triumph, Clay set his sights on the world championship.

to lose, they had the muscle to discipline rough, slum-bred fighters, bookies, fixers, and anyone else who got out of line."[21]

Gangsters maintained their stranglehold on professional boxing until the mid-fifties. In late 1956 Floyd Patterson became the heavyweight champ after Rocky Marciano retired. Former Olympian Patterson defiantly let it be known that he, not the underworld, would pick his opponents. Then, a few years later, a Supreme Court decision broke up the International Boxing Club (IBC), identified as the controlling force behind professional boxing. The IBC had been accused and found guilty of violating antitrust laws, which prohibit certain business monopolies. With the Court's ruling, boxing had, to a degree, come clean. The mob was no longer at the heart of the sport, though it still existed at the fringes.

For the fighters themselves, careers were often nightmares. Often they suffered physical damage, and usually the culprit was bad management. Managers and promoters would put profits ahead of anything else, including medical supervision of their fighters. They might push a fighter into a bout before he had time to recover sufficiently from injuries suffered in a previous bout. This was said to have happened to Benny Paret, who died at the hands of Emile Griffith in April 1962. The referee had helplessly looked on while Paret's management refused to call an end to the beating their fighter eventually succumbed to.

Because of bad management, boxers also often suffered financially. Sometimes a boxer's manager would unethically take advantage of the fighter and leave him with nothing at the end of his career. Sometimes boxers had problems with

A bloodied Benny Paret slumps to the canvas after suffering a brutal beating at the hands of Emile Griffith. When Paret later died from his injuries, many blamed his management for failing to stop the fight earlier.

money that good management could have planned for and helped avoid. Bad financial management caused Joe Louis to suffer from business losses and tax problems at the end of his life. Sugar Ray Robinson, once considered a shrewd businessman with investments that included a barber shop, a cafe, and several apartment buildings, fell into poverty late in his life, and bad management was a main cause of it. In fact, boxers who retired from the ring financially sound and who stayed that way were the exception, not the rule.

The Louisville Sponsoring Group

Cassius Clay Sr. decided he could make his son one of the exceptions by signing him

Clay and his father (far left) sign a professional contract with the Louisville Sponsoring Group in 1960, confident that the group can help the young boxer realize his goal of becoming world champion.

up with the Louisville Sponsoring Group. The group was made up of eleven wealthy white businessmen led by local sportsman Bill Favorsham. The white businessmen had the right connections, and the money, to get Clay a shot at what he wanted most—the world championship. The group saw it as a reasonable investment, given Clay's triumphant performance in the Olympics. The members of the group saw owning a piece of a prizefighter as an adventure, too. Who knew how far the talented young boxer would go in the world?

The Clay family signed a contract with the group. The Clays received a ten-thousand-dollar fee—an enormous amount for them—and the Louisville group was guaranteed 50 percent of Cassius's prize money for the next six years. Cassius himself received a four-hundred-dollar monthly allowance.

The management issue was finally settled, but Clay still needed a trainer. After a personality conflict with veteran boxer Archie Moore, who had tried training Clay in San Diego, Cassius returned to Louisville. The search for a new trainer ended with the choice of Angelo Dundee, whom Clay had met in 1955 when Clay was fifteen years old and Dundee was in Louisville getting world light middleweight champion Willie Pastrano ready for a fight. Now, five years later, Dundee and Clay immediately reestablished their relationship and began training in earnest in Miami Beach in the Fifth Street Gym.

Building a Boxer

When Cassius Clay arrived in Miami with Angelo Dundee, the young boxer weighed only 182 pounds. His physique had yet to fill out. In time, though, he would weigh 225 pounds and stand six-feet-three—fairly tall for a boxer. He trained aggressively and for long hours and learned everything he could about developing his skills—even when he hated doing something, like learning to hit the light bag, which required patience and dexterity

Practical Joker

Angelo Dundee became Clay's trainer late in 1960. Along with all the rigors of training, there was time for fun—as Dundee recalls in an article he wrote for Sports Illustrated:

"I woke up in the middle of the night and smelled smoke. I called the hotel manager and he told me nothing was wrong. I went back to sleep and woke up with the room beginning to fill with smoke. I ran out of the bedroom to wake up Ali [Clay], and he was in the living room burning a towel and fanning the smoke under the door into my bedroom. Lots of times he'd hide in a closet with a sheet over his head and jump out and holler boo at me because he knows I'm jumpy."

and which helped build timing and sharp reflexes. Indeed, his determination made him into a boxer with great skills. Dundee would later recall, "The most important thing was, he really wanted to be a fighter."[22]

Some observers thought Clay's boxing style, adopted during his first years under Joe Martin, might prevent him from being an effective fighter. Who boxed with his hands down at his hips, like Clay did? Who backed away from punches, like Clay did, instead of slipping to the side to avoid them? Clay's tactics didn't make sense. Tactics like these, the boxing observers noted, would get a fighter knocked flat on the canvas.

Clay was unconcerned about and sometimes scornful of criticism of his style, which he claimed worked just fine for him. He described his boxing style in this playful manner: "I like to hit a guy with two fast left jabs, a right cross and then a big left hook. If he's still standing after that—and if it ain't the referee that's holding him up—I runs."[23]

Dundee saw that the unorthodox style worked because of Clay's incredible quickness. Clay, fighting as a heavyweight, had

A canny and skilled trainer, Angelo Dundee (left) would remain with Clay throughout his boxing career.

Despite his unorthodox boxing style, Clay's incredible quickness in the ring often enabled him to avoid being hit.

the speed of a welterweight (a fighter under 147 pounds) and could, when he wanted, avoid being hit altogether. So the trainer quickly developed the perfect way to train the young man. For one thing, he had Clay spar, or practice, with two veterans in the Dundee camp, Willie Pastrano and the Cuban champion, Luis Manuel Rodriguez. Daily work with the two honed Clay's skills.

Second, and more importantly, Dundee realized that Clay could not be told what to do. He would not listen to direct advice. He was incredibly stubborn about changing to conform to someone else's view.

Dundee decided to instruct Clay in a roundabout way, to make Clay think he was responsible for his own improvement. If, for instance, he thought that the young boxer was throwing a left hook too high, Dundee would say, "That's great! You're really effective when you throw that hook nice and low." Clay would concentrate, then, on altering his punch, unaware that

he had been influenced by the canny Dundee's strategy.

Of course, Clay would always insist that he was solely responsible for developing his style. "When you want to talk about who made me," he said, early in his career, "you talk to me. Who made me is *me*."[24]

After the Hunsaker fight, the confident boxer made quick work of Herb Siler, Tony Esperti, and Jim Robinson. Dundee's training strategy seemed to be working well.

Dundee had another bit of strategy for the young fighter that had little to do with what went on inside the boxing ring. The lesson was on the importance of publicity and the people who provided it: "The newspaper guys, the magazine guys, the television and radio guys. I told him, 'These are your friends. This is what it's all about. They want to talk to you. Always respect that. Because when they stop talking to you, then you're a dead issue.'"[25]

One afternoon in Miami, Dundee and others at the Fifth Street Gym had a glimpse of the future. While training for a fight with Texan Donnie Fleeman—whom Clay would defeat in seven rounds—Clay learned that Ingemar Johansson, the former heavyweight champion, was in town, training for a fight with heavyweight champion Floyd Patterson. When the call went out from Johansson's camp that sparring partners were needed, Clay eagerly volunteered his services, looking delighted and saying brightly that he would go "dancin' with Johansson." Johansson's management looked at Clay as if he were crazy. They wanted a proper performance from an obedient fighter.

In Miami for publicity as well as training, Johansson didn't realize that the young boxer who faced him in the ring wanted some publicity, too. Harold Conrad, who promoted the match between Patterson and Johansson, recalled Clay's boxing performance:

Former heavyweight champion Ingemar Johansson was humiliated during a sparring session with Clay, who was able to avoid every punch Johansson threw.

They got in the ring, and Johansson had a great right hand but two left feet, and Cassius started dancing, popping him. Now remember, Johansson was getting ready to fight for the heavyweight championship of the world, but Cassius handled him like a sparring partner. . . . Johansson was furious. . . . He started chasing Clay around the ring, throwing right hands and missing by twenty feet.[26]

Clay later recalled the brief sparring session:

I sparred two rounds with Johansson in Miami and he never put a glove on me. Boy, I sure made him mad. He was so mad that he wouldn't come back to Miami as planned. He wanted me to go to Palm Beach where we could spar in private. Not me. When I work, I want the newspapermen to see me if I do anything great and sensational. By the end of the first round I had Johansson pinned against the ropes, all shook up and very mad.[27]

The Louisville Lip

Just before his fight against Hawaiian heavyweight Duke Sabedong on June 26, 1961, in Las Vegas, Clay appeared on a local radio talk show to promote the fight. While Clay said basically what was expected of him—that he was in good shape and that he believed he would be victorious—he was completely upstaged by a professional wrestler, also on the program, also promoting a match. Gorgeous George sported long golden hair, wore sequined

Playing Around

"Besmanoff rushed at Clay with such anger people thought Clay was going to get massacred. But, in reality, Besmanoff was making the night tougher on himself. . . . Every time he rushed his younger and faster opponent, Besmanoff found nothing in front of him. When he turned to look for Clay, his face had gloves all over it. In round five, Besmanoff was defenseless. But Clay wanted to fulfill his prediction. So he just moved around using his jab, while Dundee yelled at him: 'Stop playing around. Stop playing around.'

The beginning of round seven showed a different fighter. Clay came up with an aggressive attitude not shown in the previous rounds. He stalked his opponent and hit him with fast, strong jabs and followed those with straight right-hand punches. His last punch was a straight right to the jaw. Besmanoff went back, down and out. Nothing moved in his body for over ten seconds. It was a display of punching power, and of accuracy and speed while delivering the punches. 'When he was not playing around, he looked like a champ,' remembered Dundee."

capes and robes, and had a personal hairdresser who sprayed him with perfume before the start of each match. Additionally, as young Clay listened in awe, Gorgeous George did not stop at simply predicting victory. He boasted:

I am the world's greatest wrestler. I cannot be defeated. . . . Look at my velvet skin. Look at my pretty hair. If that bum messes my hair up tomorrow night I'll annihilate him. I want all of you out there to come to the Sports Palace early because I'm gonna mop the floor with this bum. If he beats me I'll cut off my golden hair and throw it out to the audience and go bald.[28]

Clay was thrilled by George's boasts. He later would claim that no matter what happened in Gorgeous George's match, he wanted to see it. And the change in Clay was evident. He immediately stepped up his own taunting of his opponents and his boasting of his abilities.

Not only did he boast and brag and insult, but he also went Gorgeous George one better: Cassius began framing his pre-

During a radio talk show Clay was upstaged by the boasting of another guest, professional wrestler Gorgeous George (right). The incident motivated Clay to escalate his own boasting and taunting before fights.

dictions in rhyme. No one in boxing had ever done anything as flamboyant as this before. In his 1961 fights against Alonzo Johnson, Alex Miteff, and Willie Besman-off, Clay, now often called the Louisville Lip, predicted each round in which he would win. "They all must fall in the round I call," he would declare. In each fight, his prediction was borne out.

In 1962 Clay continued to build his unbeaten record as a professional. Sonny Banks fell in four rounds. Don Warner and George Logan were each stopped in the fourth. Clay scored knockouts over Billy Daniels and Alejandro Lavorante. None of these boxers was a contender, but each was a bit better than the previous fighter, and this enabled Clay to improve his talents and confidence with little danger of actually losing a fight—another key strate-

gy of Dundee's for bringing a young boxer along slowly but surely.

But Clay was brimming with confidence. He maintained that he was ready for Sonny Liston, the heavyweight champion, and he was determined to let Liston and the rest of the world know it.

Sonny Liston, the dominant and most feared fighter in the heavyweight division of boxing, had a frightening reputation outside as well as inside the ring. An editorial in *Sports Illustrated* reported:

> By the time he was 18 he had been sentenced to three concurrent five-year jail terms for armed robberies. . . . In 1956 Liston beat up a St. Louis cop and took his gun away from him. He got nine months, and his boxing license was suspended in Missouri

Heavyweight champion Sonny Liston was reputed to be the most feared fighter in the heavyweight division.

for a time. Since its restoration, he has been seen in the company of known gangsters.[29]

Taunting the Champ

In July 1962, in Las Vegas, though, the upcoming return match between Liston and former champ Floyd Patterson was of secondary interest. Of primary interest was the brash young Cassius Clay's publicly taunting Liston into giving him a shot at the title. One day Clay walked into a casino where Liston was gambling. He berated the older man, calling him a "big, ugly bear" until Liston pulled out a revolver and started shooting, sending Clay and his entourage running into the street. Liston then revealed that the gun shot only blanks, and everyone had a good laugh at Clay's expense.

Another night Clay drove to Liston's exclusive neighborhood and stopped at a pay phone. He called the police and the local newspaper, telling them, anonymously, that Cassius Clay had come up to Liston's house and there was going to be a big fight. Then Clay parked in front of the house. He screamed at Liston through a megaphone, taunting him, challenging him to fight then and there. He drove off only after police and reporters had arrived. An enraged Liston found a bear trap left on his lawn. The press loved it.

At a news conference the morning after Clay appeared on Liston's front lawn, Clay boasted that he was ready to "go to war" against Liston. Recalls writer Huston Horn, "The world's meanest man [Liston] dissolved into rib-racking, eye-watering laughter. 'I'm the champ of fightin',' he spluttered, 'but you the champ of talkin'.'"[30]

Finally, Clay appeared in the ring just before the opening round of the Liston-Patterson rematch. Invited by the ring announcer and widely applauded, Clay stepped through the ropes and shook hands with challenger Patterson.

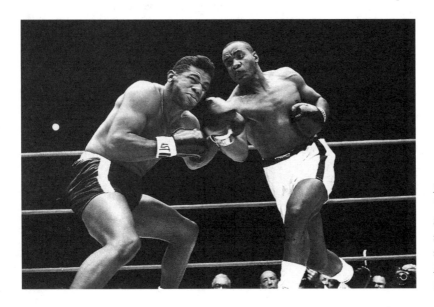

Boasting that he was ready to "go to war," Clay's public taunting of Liston succeeded in piquing more public interest than the upcoming Liston-Patterson rematch (pictured).

According to boxing custom, he should have nodded to Liston or gone over to shake his hand, then quickly left the ring. Clay, though, had his own plan. After smiling at Patterson, he turned around, looked at Liston, appeared fearful, and dashed through the ropes and out of the ring, as if fleeing for his life. The fans loved it. Clay had stolen the spotlight from the champion of the world.

Liston didn't show any pleasure in Clay's act. He concentrated on the business at hand. The bell to signal the beginning of the fight rang, and Liston knocked out Patterson in the first round—as he had in their first fight months before.

While Clay continually talked to the press of his desire to fight Liston, he was able to maintain his winning record. On November 15, 1962, he fought former light heavyweight boxing champion Archie Moore, who had earlier been hired to train the young Olympian. Though Moore was well past his prime, many boxing critics thought he could pose a problem for the younger fighter because of his vast ring experience. Clay, typically, was confident of his own abilities. Before the fight, Clay made a prediction again. At a news conference at which both boxers were present, Cassius predicted that Moore would fall in the fourth round.

"The only way I'll fall in four, Cassius," Moore replied, "is by tripping over your prostrate form."

"If I lose," said Cassius, "I'm going to crawl across the ring and kiss your feet. Then I'll leave the country."[31]

Moore fell in four.

In 1963, as in the subsequent years, each of Clay's opponents was a step up from the one before. In January Clay scored a

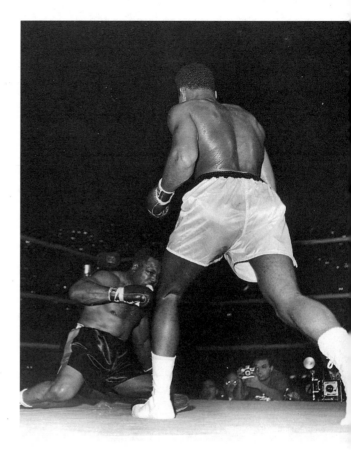

Just as he had predicted, Clay knocked out veteran boxer Archie Moore in the fourth round of their bout.

knockout over Charlie Powell in just three rounds. But on March 13 Clay had trouble with a small heavyweight named Doug Jones. Clay prevailed, though, coming out ahead on a ten-round decision.

Before the Jones fight, Clay met and hired Drew ("Bundini") Brown as a corner assistant. Bundini had worked for Sugar Ray Robinson and other fighters. Dr. Ferdie Pacheco, who would soon become Clay's ringside physician, remembers that Bundini came along at the right time in Clay's career. Pacheco says that Clay was still an innocent kid who needed someone else's harsh experience with life to learn from. Bundini, recalls Pacheco, "was a consummate street artist . . . street-smart and tough on one side, sweet, sensitive, and loving on the other. . . . Never has a professor had a more attentive student."[32]

Bundini, loud, brash, and eccentric, was to be the creator of the war cry most associated with the future champion:

> Float like a butterfly,
> Sting like a bee,
> Rumble, young man, rumble,
> Aaaaaaaaaaaaagh![33]

Before his June 8, 1963, fight in London against British champion Henry Cooper, Clay donned a regal robe and declared himself the king of boxing. He insisted that he alone was fit for the crown, and that others—like Liston—were mere pretenders. The crowd cheered in appreciation of the young American's sense of play.

In the ring against Cooper, though, Clay was knocked off his throne. Cooper, though initially cut around the eyes from Clay's sharp and probing jabs, caught Clay by surprise with a left hook in the fourth round that knocked the young fighter down and through the ropes. It would be one of the few times Clay was knocked off his feet. Dazed, Clay was saved by the bell at the end of the fourth round, while the hometown crowd roared and cheered for Cooper. But after a prolonged rest—because of a split seam in Clay's boxing glove, which took an extra minute or two to repair—Clay came back strong in the next round. He hammered away almost vengefully at Cooper's wounded face,

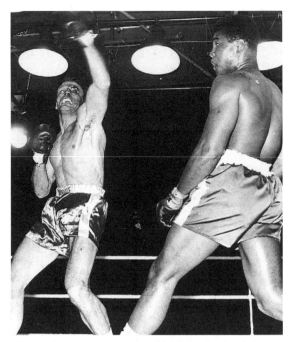

Henry Cooper attempts a wild left hook after being badly wounded on the face by Clay. Clay came back strong to win the fight in the fifth round, after recovering from a fourth-round knockdown.

sending blood flying everywhere. The referee finally intervened and awarded the fight to Clay.

After the fight Clay received a pleasant surprise. Sonny Liston's manager had flown from America to deliver a message from the champ. It contained some helpful advice, the mistaken presumption that Clay was a married man, and an ominous prediction: "Please drink your orange juice and your milk shakes. Stay well and healthy. You talked yourself into a World Heavyweight Title fight. Now your wife can be a rich widow."[34]

3 A New Champion for a New Decade

During the first three years of the 1960s, while young Cassius Clay, now a professional fighter, was busy establishing a string of unbeaten performances, America found itself moving forward and back between hope and sadness. The election of President John F. Kennedy ushered in a spirit of social change, and Americans believed their country could be a shining light of democracy for the world. Numerous demonstrations for civil rights culminated in the spirited March on Washington, where Martin Luther King Jr. and other African-American leaders joined almost half a million marchers calling for peace and equality in the land. America was surely on the right track and could even lead the way abroad, by helping people fight against communism in a little country called Vietnam, on the other side of the globe.

But then came the assassination of the young president in November 1963. The nation mourned. In this time of sadness many people turned their attention to other national obsessions that offered more joy than politics did—such as sports. Sports had no politics, no assassinations. They simply represented a pure drive for excellence that sports fans could share with their favorite athletes. Many Americans, in the wake of the Kennedy assassination, found among the rising young sports stars an exuberant, immensely talented Cassius Clay. Having been victorious in all nineteen of his professional fights, Clay was now in training for his chance at the World Boxing Association heavyweight championship title, held by the fearsome Charles "Sonny" Liston.

Martin Luther King Jr. helps lead the March on Washington in 1963. Clay's rise as a professional boxer came at a turbulent time in America's history.

"Exactly the Way I Planned It"

Just before the first Liston fight Clay wrote an article in Sports Illustrated *called "I'm a Little Special." He was as honest then as in later years about the reasons for his boasting and bragging:*

"Where do you think I'd be next week if I didn't know how to shout and holler and make the public sit up and take notice? I would be poor, for one thing, and I would probably be down in Louisville, Kentucky, my home town, washing windows or running an elevator and saying 'yes suh' and 'no suh' and knowing my place. Instead of that, I'm saying I'm one of the highest-paid athletes in the world, which is true, and that I'm the greatest fighter in the world, which I hope and pray is true. Now the public has heard me talk enough and they're saying to me, 'Put up or shut up.' This fight with Liston is truly a command performance. And that's exactly the way I planned it."

Sonny Liston agreed to fight Cassius Clay in Miami on February 25, 1964, and the overwhelming consensus was that Liston would destroy the cocky young fighter. Much of the boxing world actually questioned Clay's sanity in wanting to get in the ring with Liston. Writer Huston Horn reported that "Rocky Marciano hinted Clay ought to have his beautiful head examined, and a California boxing expert . . . said the fight 'is a mismatch of the first magnitude.'"[35] Writer Robert H. Boyle wrote that "Clay's style is made to order for another massacre."[36]

Boxing writers saw no flaws in Liston. After watching him dispose of former champion Floyd Patterson in one round, writer Boyle noted that Liston "is huge yet lithe, a rare blending of strength, balance, and reflexes."[37] Further, Boyle described Liston as "a virtually indestructible and demonstrably deadly fighting machine

. . . an opponent with endurance, highly developed skills, deceptive speed and strength enough to stun an elephant with either hand."[38]

Odds Against Clay

As a challenger back in the early 1960s, Liston had been open to the media and the public accepted him, with his up-from-nothing beginnings, as an underdog. But after having won the title by a one-round knockout of Floyd Patterson in 1962, his attitude changed. He became openly hostile and spoke venomously to the press and fans alike. The public soured toward him, and reference was made to his connection with underworld figures. America had turned against him. His new image was that of an unpredictable, angry, powerful force. Norman Mailer said of Liston, "One held one's breath when near him."[39]

While most Americans were happily behind brash young Cassius Clay, the odds against his beating Sonny Liston were formidable. No one in the media really gave him a chance. Las Vegas odds maker Jimmy "the Greek" Snyder, famous for his accuracy, gave Clay an 8-to-1 chance of beating Liston. "It's impossible for Clay to last six rounds," said Snyder.[40]

Clay, though, protested claims of Liston's invincibility. He vowed not to stand still and be a target for Liston, as Floyd Patterson had been. Clay planned to dance: "Have you ever seen a mirage on the desert?" he asked in an article he wrote for *Sports Illustrated* before the fight. "You walk along looking for a drink of water, and suddenly you see a lake and you jump in. All you get is a mouthful of sand. Mr. Liston will get a mouthful of leather the same way."[41]

Despite his brave front, he was concerned about his chances of winning, and he welcomed support from anyone who could help him. One of the most surprising sources was Malcom X, the controversial African-American leader. Clay had invited him and his family to Miami as Clay's guests.

His connection with Malcom X caused a rumor that Cassius Clay was a member of the Black Muslims, a name given by the media to a black Islamic group called the Nation of Islam. This rumor almost stopped the fight. The Nation of Islam, in the eyes of the American public, was a radical political group espousing racial hatred and segregation.

Suddenly Cassius Clay's popularity fell. Ticket sales for the fight plummeted. The promoter, Bill MacDonald, actually cancelled the fight when Clay refused to go in front of the media and renounce any connection with the Nation of Islam.

"That ape is almost as ugly as Sonny," jeers Clay to a costumed circus clown. Despite his public bravado, few believed that Clay had a chance of beating Liston.

Clay's association with African-American leader Malcolm X (left) caused the boxer's popularity to plummet, almost resulting in the cancellation of the Liston-Clay match.

MacDonald insisted that this was what the American public wanted. Clay, though, did not budge. There was a standoff, and Clay's camp began packing their bags. At the last moment MacDonald agreed to make a concession: Clay's renouncement of Islam was not mandatory. This satisfied Clay; the fight was on again.

The Nation of Islam

The Nation of Islam had caused controversy since its inception. The Lost-Found Nation of Islam, later simply the Nation of Islam, had its origin in the 1930s with the arrival in Detroit of a man named Fard. Fard told his closest followers that he was Mahdi, or God, and that he was on a divine mission to teach black Americans about their African and Islamic heritage. Fard claimed that blacks were the first

people to rule the world and would soon rule it again.

In the 1930s Fard met a small, frail Detroit autoworker named Elijah Poole. Fard changed Poole's life. Poole was awed by Fard and recognized some great power the other man had. Fard took Poole on as a disciple, taught him the beliefs of what he called the Lost-Found Nation of Islam, then renamed him Elijah Muhammad and designated him his one and only prophet.

The Nation of Islam had at its core the belief that black people were the original people on earth, but that they had been supplanted by evil whites. However, they would return soon in a preordained Armageddon (a great, final confrontation between Good and Evil) and would once again rule the world.

For the most part members followed beliefs of traditional Islam, a religion rooted in the Middle East. All members were taught to abstain from pork, tobacco, and alcohol, and to practice thriftiness and cleanliness. Women had second-class status.

While Fard's teachings borrowed heavily from traditional Islam, there were a few outstanding distinctions. Traditional Islam has Muhammad, a seventh-century visionary, as its one and only prophet; Fard, claiming to be God, named Elijah Muhammad his prophet. Traditional Islam teaches love and brotherhood among all the races; Fard believed that whites could not be loved, for they were devils.

In the time Fard and Muhammad worked together—until Fard's mysterious disappearance in 1934—they managed to raise the membership in the Nation of Islam to about eight thousand. Elijah Muhammad stayed at the helm as the years passed and membership went up and down. Occasionally the group was in

Clay and his brother Rudy (left) meet with Nation of Islam prophet Elijah Muhammad (center). Clay's association with the controversial black group caused a public uproar.

the public eye; more often, it went about its business without recognition or acclaim in corners of the North's urban ghettos. Its message, though, always remained the same: the white man is the Devil.

National attention riveted on the Nation in 1959 when journalist Mike Wallace produced a documentary called "The Hate That Hate Produced." White viewers around the country were shocked to discover the teachings of the Nation of Islam and its ideals, which included segregation of the races.

The Rise of Malcolm X

At the end of the 1950s white America had another reason to be concerned about the Nation, and that was the rise to prominence of its chief spokesperson and minister, Malcolm X.

Malcolm Little, born in Omaha, Nebraska, had been a petty criminal and street hustler in Boston and Harlem. He landed in jail. There he discovered and accepted Islam and changed his name from Malcolm Little to Malcolm X. The X stood for his true name, which he did not know and which had been replaced by the surname given his family by "white oppressors" generations ago. Malcolm X was a great speaker and converted many people to the Nation. He had been the obvious favorite of Elijah Muhammad since Malcolm's release from prison. However, in 1964, Malcolm X had been banned from the Nation. He had uttered public remarks making light of President Kennedy's assassination the preceding November, and he was being punished. But the real reason for his punishment, many believed, was because of his power and influence in the Nation, which threatened the standing of Elijah Muhammad himself.

Though he knew it might cause public uproar, Clay had invited Malcolm X, whom he had met a couple of years before, and his family to escape controversy for awhile, vacationing in Miami and spending time at Clay's training camp. Malcolm X was glad for the opportunity to be away from the turmoil in his public life and did his best to encourage Clay about the fight with Liston during the last few days before the fight. Malcolm X's presence offstage was perceived by the media as a sign that the young Olympian was hanging around with a bad crowd.

Crazy Clay?

Either before or during the visit of Malcolm X, Clay, who had been searching desperately for a flaw in Liston's armor, found what he had been looking for. Clay received word that during Liston's time in prison, Liston had feared one thing—crazy people. Sane people could be intimidated; they understood the threat of force. But crazy people were unpredictable. They might do anything.

The weigh-in revealed a "crazy" Cassius Clay. After Liston stepped off the scales, in came the challenger's entourage, led by an arm-waving, insult-yelling Cassius Clay with Bundini by his side. "Float like butterfly, sting like a bee," they chanted, making their way down to Liston. Arriving at the scales, Clay insulted Liston and lunged at him time and again, though managing to be held back by his crew. He ranted and raved at a fever pitch, and his blood pressure, measured by a boxing official, reflected his hysteria: it was over two hundred. The fight was nearly called off because of this. The doctors agreed, though, to take Clay's blood pressure a little later, when he was calmer and apparently not so frightened.

Clay is restrained after repeatedly lunging at challenger Liston during weigh-in ceremonies. Clay staged his "crazy" antics in an effort to unnerve Liston.

During Clay's fit of hysteria, Liston stood calmly, staring silently. But Clay was having an effect on the champion. Angelo Dundee, who had been in the Ali entourage, later recalled:

Liston changed right there. Liston completely changed, because a tough guy is always afraid of a crazy guy. Liston really thought this kid was crazy, yelling "I'm going to get you" and pretending he wanted to fight Liston right there. What nobody noticed was, I'm holding him back with one finger in his chest. One finger.[42]

Clay and his entourage left the arena as noisily as they had entered it. About thirty minutes later, away from the media and the cameras, Clay had his blood pressure checked again. It was normal.

Clay was relaxed the day of the fight—February 25, 1964. One would expect that during the final hours before the title fight, while the preliminary bouts took place, Clay would be in his dressing room praying or meditating or going over strategy with his trainers and manager. But at this time his concerns were not entirely with the biggest fight of his career. His brother Rudy was fighting in a preliminary match, and Cassius came out of the dressing room and stood in the aisle, cheering his brother on. The bout was mismatched; Rudy was taking a beating, and Cassius was crying. "My brother ain't never going to fight again," he vowed.[43] Then he went back to the dressing room for final preparations for the biggest fight of his life.

The first few rounds were even. Clay was careful to keep away from Liston's powerful left hook. Liston plodded after Clay, who kept him confused with rapid-fire jabs to the head. By the third round, Clay's jabs had opened a cut under Liston's left eye, but the champion remained undaunted; he moved forward, trying to trap Clay on the ropes, waiting for a chance to shut the young challenger's mouth with a solid knockout punch.

As the fifth round got underway, Clay was suddenly in trouble. He kept rubbing at his eyes and looking wildly to his corner for help. Liniment from Liston's sore shoulder had found its way into Clay's eyes, which burned and stung and teared. Partially blinded, he kept out of the frustrated Liston's reach for most of the round.

Psychological Warfare

Near the end of that round, though, Clay seemed to recover. As his concentration

---

Psychological Knots

Norman Mailer has written much about Muhammad Ali. Here, in his essay titled "King of the Hill," from Reading the Fights, *Mailer talks about one of young Cassius Clay's greatest boxing weapons:*

"A man in the ring is a performer as well as a gladiator. Elaborating his technique from the age of twelve, Clay knew how to work on the vanity of other performers, knew how to make them feel ridiculous and so force them into crucial mistakes, knew how to set such a tone from the first round—later he was to know how to begin it a year before he would even meet the man. Clay knew that a fighter who had been put in psychological knots before he got near the ring had already lost half, three-quarters, no, all of the fight could be lost before the first punch. That was the psychology of the body."

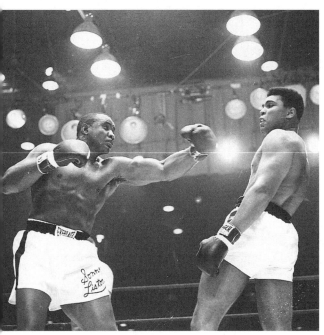

Clay deftly avoids Liston's powerful left hook. Using "psychological warfare" tactics, Clay sought to destroy Liston's concentration in the fifth round.

returned, he sought to destroy Liston's. Writer Tex Maule describes how Clay, with a classic manuever, took control of the bout:

> He reached out a long left hand and held it on Sonny's head. Liston, tired and dispirited after having chased the nimble Clay fruitlessly for almost three minutes, stood transfixed, as a bull is mesmerized after a matador has controlled him with a series of passes. Finally it was Clay who broke the weird tableau. He took his hand away and slapped Liston five or six times on the forehead like a man knocking on a door, before he danced away.[44]

This was another form of Clay's psychological warfare, about which writer Norman Mailer commented, "Clay knew how to work on the vanity of other performers, knew how to make them feel ridiculous and so force them into crucial mistakes."[45]

The bell rang and Clay returned to his corner. He pawed at his eyes. He squinted and grimaced. He wanted to quit, and he asked Dundee to cut his boxing gloves off. Dundee calmly reminded him that this was the big fight, and at the sound of the bell Dundee pushed Clay off his stool and toward the middle of the ring.

Champion of the World

Though his eyes were still blurry and burning, Clay came out for the sixth round like a hurricane. He attacked Liston from many angles, as if in desperation. Liston was overwhelmed, and he was suffering from the sore shoulder and the cut under his eye. At the end of the round Clay returned to his corner, clearly the round's winner. Liston slumped in his own corner. When the bell rang to begin the seventh round, Liston did not rise. Due to injuries, he was unable to continue. Quite suddenly, Cassius Clay was the champion of the world.

In the ring reporters shoved and jockeyed for position. All had an idea of what Clay would have to say now, after all the talk of becoming champ, after all the bragging and boasting, after having actually beaten terrible Sonny Liston, against everyone's odds. Clay, true to his flamboyant image, did not disappoint them:

> I knew I had him in the first round. Almighty God was with me. I want everybody to bear witness. I am the greatest! I shook up the world! I'm the greatest thing that ever lived. I don't

Against everyone's odds, Clay defeated the formidable Liston for the world heavyweight title. Trainers Dundee and Brown look on as Clay raises his hands in celebration of victory.

have a mark on my face, and I upset Sonny Liston, and I just turned twenty-two years old. I must be the greatest. I showed the world, I talk to God every day. I shook up the world. I'm the king of the world! I'm pretty! I'm a bad man! I shook up the world! I shook up the world! I shook up the world! You must listen to me. I am the greatest! I can't be beat! I am the greatest! It was no match. I want the world to know, I'm so great that Sonny Liston was not even a match. I don't have a mark on my face. In the fifth round, I couldn't see a thing. My face was burning, and I whupped him. He couldn't hurt me. I'm the prettiest thing that ever lived. I shook up the world. I want justice.[46]

A New Name and Identity

The morning after the fight, the young world champion had more announcements to make. The media gathered as Clay announced that he had become a Muslim. Then he announced that his new name was Muhammad Ali, a name conferred upon him by Nation of Islam leader Elijah Muhammad, who had called in the wake of the victory and officially accepted the boxer into the Nation. *Muhammad*, Ali told reporters, means "one worthy of praise." *Ali* was the name of a great soldier related to the Islamic prophet Muhammad.

Ali insisted that he and Nation of Islam members were not "Black Muslims"—

True to his flamboyant image Clay boasts to reporters "I am the greatest! I can't be beat!" following his triumph over Liston. The following day Clay announced that he had adopted the Muslim name Muhammad Ali.

at least, that name was not chosen by them: "I am not a Black Muslim," said Ali, "because that is a word made up by the white press. I am a black man who has adopted Islam."[47]

He became defensive as reporters questioned him about his religion:

> I believe in Allah [Islam's supreme being, or God] and in peace. What's wrong with that? I don't try to move into white neighborhoods. I don't want to marry a white woman. I don't want to hurt no one like the Ku Klux Klan. I was baptized when I was twelve, but I didn't know what I was doing. I'm not a Christian anymore.[48]

The response of the press to his new name and identity was tumultuous. Ali recalls the piercing words of contempt that poured from columns in the nation's newspapers:

> William F. Buckley, Jr., pleaded for "someone to succeed in knocking sense into Clay's head before he's done damaging the sport." Jimmy

Breslin described me as a "Muslim and a bedbug." Jimmy Cannon stated that boxing was better off being run by the Mafia than by the Black Muslims. "The heavyweight champion is the symbol of masculinity and youth of America," one columnist wrote. "If so, it has now descended into the darkest dungeons of hell, into the worse worms of race hate and degradation, worse than when it was controlled by . . . gangsters . . . [who] were sweet angels to the people who control Muhammad Ali."[49]

If America, speaking through its journalists, was shocked and angered at Clay's announcement, other parts of the world took the news of the boxer's new identity in stride, or even with a sense of pride and joy. The declaration of his new identity as a Muslim boosted his popularity immensely, especially in Muslim countries and populations that would otherwise never have heard of or taken an interest in him. He had gone beyond the boundaries of the country he was born in and captured the imagination of the world.

Second Chance for Liston

On May 25, 1965, Muhammad Ali met Sonny Liston in Lewiston, Maine, in a rematch. Tension hung over the arena that night. Malcolm X had been assassinated in February—many believed Elijah Muhammad had given the order—and there was fear that Ali, who had taken Elijah Muhammad's side in his dispute with Malcolm X, might himself be the target of a reprisal by Malcolm's followers. Most in the arena that night—including Sonny Liston—were unnerved, but Ali seemed calm and in control of himself.

This second fight between Liston and Ali was to be perhaps the most controversial fight in boxing history. In the first round, Ali hit Liston with a quick right to the head, and Liston went down—and the fight was suddenly over. There have been various opinions about the famous "phantom punch." Boxing critics still claim that the punch was powerless and Liston went down on purpose—that he had thrown the fight. But Angelo Dundee strongly disagrees: "There was a punch, a good right hand to the temple my guy threw from up on the balls of his feet. I saw the punch. Lots of people saw the punch. The thing is, Liston never saw the punch."[50]

The two losses to Ali seemed to take the heart out of Sonny Liston. Liston fought for a few more years, though never again as a major contender. Six years after his second defeat at the hands of Ali, Liston was to appear before a Senate subcommittee in Washington to testify about what he knew regarding the involvement of organized crime in the boxing world. Liston never got the opportunity to testify. He was found

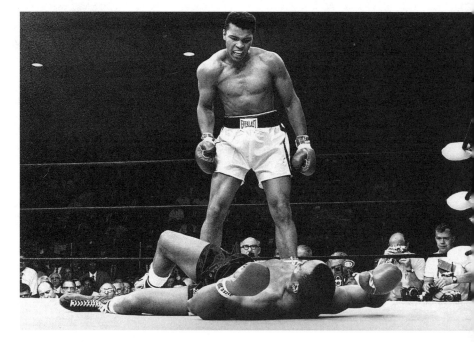

Ali taunts Liston to get up after knocking him out in the first round of their 1965 rematch. Many boxing critics believe that the punch was powerless and Liston went down on purpose—that he had thrown the fight.

dead in his Las Vegas home on January 5, 1971. Though no one thought he was involved with drugs, a hypodermic needle and heroin were found in his kitchen.

A Doomed Marriage, A New Identity

Soon after winning the heavyweight championship, Muhammad Ali married for the first time. His wife was Sonji Roi, a model and cocktail waitress who had a child from her first marriage. Many advised Ali against the marriage but he was in love. The marriage, as many predicted, did in fact dissolve less than a year later, apparently because Sonji was not active enough in her devotions to Islam.

While many journalists were skeptical of everything the flamboyant fighter did and said and suspected self-promotion as Ali's chief motive, his Muslim identity was important to Muhammad Ali. Author Robert Lipsyte provides insight:

Ali's marriage to model Sonji Roi dissolved after less than a year, reportedly because of her lack of devotion to Islam.

Ali launches a verbal attack on a smug Floyd Patterson after he refused to call him by his Muslim name.

There is no way to measure a religious experience, nor to what extent a believer invests his religion with just those attributes he wants to derive from it. Ali entered the Muslims looking for a peace and order in his world, a shield from hurt, a greater truth through divinity, a mythology, a language, a surrogate family. Whether or not they were there, he found them.[51]

He also found a measure of respect. After fighting six exhibition bouts in July and August 1965, he faced Floyd Patterson in Las Vegas on November 22, 1965. Patterson had called Ali's affiliation with the Nation of Islam a disgrace to boxing and refused to call the champion by his Muslim name. Ali, though angry, insisted that he would not make any personal statements disparaging Patterson. In the ring, though, the champion punished Patterson for twelve rounds until the referee stopped the fight. Afterwards, Patterson made a courteous and dignified statement to the media: "I was beaten by a great fighter, Muhammad Ali."[52]

4 "Ain't Got No Quarrel"

After his introduction to the principles and doctrines of the Nation of Islam in 1962, Muhammad Ali gave them a bit of thought and did not hesitate to inform the media of what some of those principles and doctrines were.

Ali had admittedly not thought too hard, though, about the Vietnam War. He looked to the newspapers and television only for news of himself. Besides, he had always been too busy training to become the heavyweight boxing champion of the world and learning about the Nation to pay serious attention to anything else. The Nation of Islam viewed the Vietnam War with contempt, calling it a white man's war fought by black men—this much Ali surely knew.

Still, people were surprised to hear how little else the boxing champ knew about Vietnam. It seemed that the whole country was wrapped up in its feelings about the Vietnam War.

The conflict in Vietnam started out as a civil war. The mid-1950s marked the end of nearly one hundred years of Western rule in Vietnam. In 1954 French colonial

Ali (seen here addressing a Nation of Islam conference) sided with the Nation on their condemnation of the Vietnam War, and would later suffer severe criticism for refusing to accept military induction.

In 1961 America joined South Vietnam in opposing the Vietcong, led by communist leader Ho Chi Minh (pictured).

forces were defeated by Vietnamese nationalists, led by Ho Chi Minh. Later that year at the Geneva Conference, French and Vietminh (Vietnamese under Ho Chi Minh) representatives were urged by delegations from Western Europe, Russia, China, and the United States to reach some kind of settlement. They agreed that Vietnam would be partitioned until elections could be held within two years to decide a single leader to rule a unified Vietnam.

Many held the opinion that Ho Chi Minh would handily win any election. This opinion was not lost on the United States and other Western powers concerned with keeping communism out of Vietnam. No election was held. Instead, South Vietnam, strongly supported by the United States and led by newly installed president Ngo Dinh Diem, declared independence from the north. Soon afterwards the south took up arms against the north, which was led by Ho's communist government and defended by his fighters, called the Vietcong.

American Intervention

American military involvement in the Vietnam War began in 1961. When Vietcong rebels in the south of the country began fighting against the South Vietnamese government, American advisors and weapons entered the war, and full-scale bombing of North Vietnamese targets came shortly afterwards. The American public was behind this intervention. Americans wanted to save the Vietnamese people from communism. They thought that with U.S. assistance the South Vietnamese army could easily defeat the relatively small Vietcong forces.

By the second half of 1963 President Kennedy was contemplating the dangers of staying too long in Vietnam. He was concerned that while American aid went to the South Vietnamese leaders, most of the aid was lost or misused by corrupt Vietnamese government officials. He thought that if American aid were used correctly, the South Vietnamese could quickly defeat their outnumbered foes. Regarding future American involvement in Vietnam, Kennedy was of two minds. He increased the number of American troops committed to Vietnam, yet he also created plans for an American withdrawal. Before he could point America's strategy clearly one way or another, though, he was assassinated in November 1963.

The new president, Lyndon B. Johnson, tried to focus his governing efforts primarily on domestic matters, but soon after assuming the role of president he became bogged down in the conflict in Vietnam. He thought it best to win the war as quickly as possible, and after a North Vietnamese attack on two American ships in the Gulf of Tonkin in July 1964, Congress gave the green light to U.S. troop involvement. After initial deployments, increasing numbers of American troops began arriving in Vietnam in 1965.

By 1966, despite the steadily increasing number of American troop deaths, the majority of American citizens still supported or at least accepted American involvement in the Vietnam War. For most, there were at least two strong reasons for supporting the war. One was that America was helping the South Vietnamese fight for their freedom against the communist-backed North Vietnamese, and the spread of communism was a great fear to most Americans. The second reason was simpler: American troops were in Vietnam, and most Americans felt that those who loved their country should support their armed forces and even serve with them if called to.

Of course, not everyone supported the war. The relatively few American individuals and groups at this time protesting American involvement in the war gathered on campuses and held small antiwar rallies. They argued that it was not our war—the United States was not under military attack. To some Americans the North Vietnamese were popular heroes—underdogs—struggling bravely against the

Unpredictable

While Cassius Clay had, as he himself put it, "shocked the world" with his knockout of Sonny Liston for the world's heavyweight boxing crown, it was not just his skill as a boxer that shocked white America, as Edna and Art Rust Jr. in their book, Art Rust's Illustrated History of the Black Athlete, *report:*

"Now a new twenty-two-year-old heavyweight champion with a new name, Muhammad Ali, and a new religion, Islam, was ready to take on the world. With his classic dimensions contained in a six-foot, three-inch frame, weighing 225 pounds, and with his undeniable speed of hands and feet, there was still doubt. Many reporters and sports figures refused to call him Muhammad Ali. To many, there was something frightening about his changes—he was not like most American blacks, as many thought they knew them. He was unpredictable. Despite the oppression and subjugation inflicted upon the blacks by the white majority, whites could not tolerate someone who dared to be different, who dared to have the courage of his convictions without the establishment's sanction."

President Lyndon B. Johnson greets American troops in Vietnam. Hoping to end the war quickly, Johnson and Congress gave the green light for U.S. troop involvement in Vietnam in 1964.

mighty forces of the United States. And many protesters argued that no war could be justified.

The Draft

The possibility of being drafted was in the mind of every young American male. Periodically the government conducted lotteries. If a young man's number was called, he had to go for a series of physical, mental, and psychological tests that usually resulted in induction into the armed forces. Most inductees were sent off to fight the war in Vietnam.

While most young men were classified 1A, which meant "fit for duty," some were able to legally avoid the draft. If, for example, a young man attended college, he was designated 2S and was excused from service; one who failed the physical or mental tests was given a 1Y rating; 4F was a general designation meaning "unfit for duty."

Members of some religious groups, such as Quakers, were able to refuse induction. They were classified as conscientious objectors. According to the law that conferred this status upon them, being conscientious objectors meant that they opposed any and all wars, that their opposition was based on religious beliefs, and that their opposition was sincere.

Rather than face induction or a prison sentence, some of those protesters who were not allowed to legally avoid the draft left American society. Many young war protesters remained in this country but took on assumed names and lived in hiding from the government. Others quietly moved to Canada and other foreign countries, leaving their country, friends, and families behind.

Until early 1966 Muhammad Ali's draft status kept him from being inducted. On March 26, 1964, the Selective Service, in charge of military draft registration, had classified him 1Y, or "legally incompetent." Ali had had a problem with the writing

Ali reports for pre-induction testing. Initially the Selective Service classified Ali as "legally incompetent" because of his difficulty with the writing portion of the test.

portion of the tests. When news of this was reported by the press before the Liston fight, Ali was embarrassed, but he put a good face on it: "I said I was the Greatest, not the smartest."[53] Politicians and reporters alike wondered aloud, though, how a man so talented and superior in his field and with the ability to compose poetry on the spot could be unacceptable material for the military. But the Selective Service had made its decision, and its decision was final.

Until 1966, that is. In February of that year, a new draft ruling made Ali eligible for the draft. In need of more soldiers, the armed forces had lowered standards to allow more young men to be drafted into the expanding war effort, and Ali was among many young Americans to have his status suddenly changed. He immediately appealed for conscientious objector status but was denied it by the Selective Service. Instead of 1Y, he was 1A and eligible for induction into the armed forces.

Outrage

Ali heard the news of his reclassification from reporters while he was in Miami training to defend his title against Ernie Terrell, set for Comiskey Park in Chicago.

He understood then that he would soon be asked to go to an induction center to be drafted. He was in shock, then the shock turned to outrage. Why had the government considered him mentally incompetent for two years, he yelled to reporters, but now thought him fully fit for battle, without having retested him? He was distressed. He had been caught by surprise by the news; reporters pressured him into expressing his emotions.

They asked him his opinion of the war. Ali responded that he did not really even know where on the map the war was taking place. They asked him if he really wanted the North Vietnamese to conquer the South Vietnamese and install their communist government throughout the entire country. Ali thought hard, hesitated, and finally shrugged. "I ain't got no quarrel with them Vietcong," he said.[54]

Ali's remark became a front-page headline in newspapers across the country. Journalists and politicians severely criticized him. One writer grouped him with "the unwashed punks" who protested the war. Another writer accused him of boasting of his fighting skills but "squealing like a rat" when asked to fight for his country. *New York Times* columnist Arthur Daly accused Ali of

> spurning patriotism and affronting a nation. . . . Clay could have been the most popular of all champions, but he attached himself to a hate organization and antagonized everyone with his boasting and his disdain for the decency of even a low-grade patriotism.[55]

Politicians were also quick to denounce Ali for his remarks. Speaking before Congress, Representative Frank Clark of Pennsylvania used a strong comparison to scold Ali for refusing to accept induction: "To welch or back off from that commitment is as unthinkable as surrendering to Adolf Hitler or Mussolini would have been in my days of military service."[56] Southern congressman Joe Waggoner called Ali a phony: "He knows it, the Supreme Court knows it, and everyone else knows it."[57] The Kentucky State Senate passed a resolution condemning Ali for his attitude, which they felt discredited all Kentuckians who had given their lives for their country.

Boxing greats from the past put their two cents in, too. Gene Tunney sent Ali a telegram warning him to apologize for his remark or be banned from the ring. Jack Dempsey spoke in the newspapers: "Muhammad Ali is finished as a fighter. Regardless of the outcome of his next fight, he is finished. He should be careful. It's not safe for him to be on the streets."[58]

Ali's Popularity Plummets

Ali's popularity in this country plummeted. "I ain't got no quarrel with them Vietcong" was plastered all over the country's newspapers and magazines, where commentators took Ali to task for his antiwar sentiments. The phrase would in fact become the slogan for draft resistors throughout the end of the decade, when protest was at its fiercest. But in the early months of 1966 it was used to show that

Relaxing before an upcoming bout, Ali points to a newspaper headline to show that he is not the only one protesting the Vietnam War.

Muhammad Ali, the heavyweight boxing champion of the world, was a dangerous person, a bad apple, a villain who would influence a generation of American children away from fighting for their country.

Parents especially saw Ali as a treacherous and direct threat. While thousands of other individuals requested conscientious objector status during the Vietnam War, and while many young people spoke out against the war in protest and marched in the streets, Muhammad Ali was from the world of sports, where everyone played more or less by the rules and tried to be good examples to the legions of youth who idolized them. Ali was, to many parents, a scoundrel who might turn their children away from loving their country.

Ali really did not have a model among former African-American athletes to guide him. Black athletes did not have a history of protesting their country's wars. Joe Louis had served proudly in the army as a morale booster, fighting exhibition matches and

Heavyweight champion Joe Louis served proudly in the U.S. Army during World War II.

making personal appearances at military bases around the world. While Jackie Robinson had nearly been court-martialed over a racial incident in the same war, he served with distinction and never had regrets about fighting for his country.

Ali had the strong support of African-American civil rights leaders, though. Martin Luther King Jr., Harlem congressman Adam Clayton Powell, and Georgia legislator Julian Bond, among others, stood behind Ali, acknowledging him as a fine example of black manhood taking a principled stand against an unjust cause.

Ali vowed to appeal for a reclassification. He told his lawyers that he wanted to get conscientious objector status. He based his request, in a letter to the authorities, on the grounds that he was a minister in the Nation of Islam, and that "to bear arms or kill is against my religion. And I conscientiously object to any combat military service that involves the participation in any war in which the lives of human beings are being taken."[59]

He also vowed that whether or not his appeal for classification was met, he would simply not be involved in the war in any capacity. And he also made it clear that no one—including Elijah Muhammad—had instructed him to take this stand. Elijah Muhammad had merely advised him to follow his own conscience.

Forced Out of the Country

After he refused to apologize publicly to the Illinois Athletic Commission for his remarks, Ali's upcoming fight with Ernie Terrell in Chicago was canceled. Ali and his managers were astounded that this organization, which had as its main function the licensing of fighters, should demand an apology. State athletic commissions were supposed to give out licenses to fight, not for what people were to think.

Other sites were considered for a Terrell-Ali match, but other state athletic commissions around the nation followed Chicago's lead. Finally, because no American city would sanction a fight in which he was involved, Ali was forced to fight his next four bouts outside of the country. Terrell, wanting no more of the Ali controversy, pulled out of a scheduled bout in Toronto, Canada.

George Chuvalo became Ali's opponent in Toronto, and on March 29, 1966, Ali defeated Chuvalo in a fifteen-round decision. In London on May 21 Ali knocked out Henry Cooper for the second

George Chuvalo (left) became Ali's opponent in Canada after Ernie Terrell pulled out of a scheduled bout to avoid controversy.

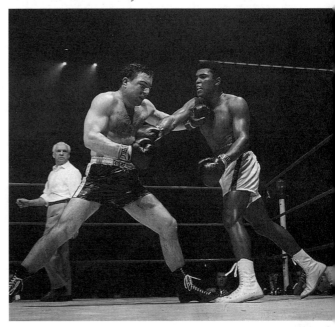

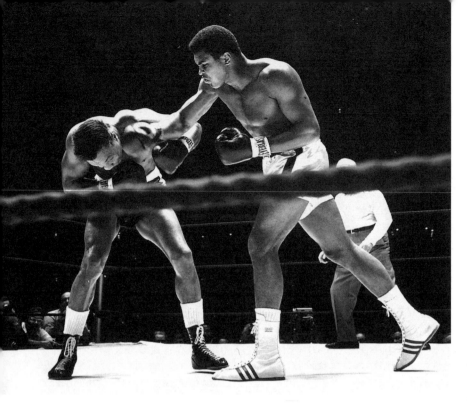

Many boxing critics consider Ali's 1966 bout with Cleveland Williams to be his greatest performance ever.

time, this time in the sixth round. On August 6, back in England, he knocked out Brian London. Finally, he defeated Karl Mildenberger in Frankfurt, Germany, in twelve rounds.

During this time Ali's contract with the Louisville Sponsoring Group ran out, and Herbert Muhammad, son of Elijah Muhammad, became his manager. Completely aligning himself now with the Nation of Islam, Ali seemed to be turning his back on the white establishment.

Clowning Around

Though concerned by what the future held for him, he was still able to clown around. After a vigorous workout while preparing for the Chuvalo fight, he put on his white robe and had fun with the fans who had crowded into the gym to watch him train. *New York Times* reporter Gerald Eskenazi recalled the lighthearted occasion, which began with Ali's demanding of the crowd,

> "Do they love me in Barbados?"
> The Barbados contingent in the crowd answered "yes." He got the same reaction when he asked for people from England, and from Trinidad, and from Jamaica.
> "I'm from Israel," shouted a ringsider.
> "Well am I the champ in Israel?"
> "No."
> "Well, you better be good, you are the only Israeli here."
> At one point in his routine, a woman shouted, "Champ, this man next to me wants to get into the ring with you."
> "Mister," said Clay, "you'd rather be in Vietnam with a BB gun."[60]

Back in the USA

Suddenly in the fall of 1966 Ali received word that he would be allowed to fight again in the United States. While the real reason for this sudden ruling change remains in doubt, author Robert Lipsyte suggests that government officials were perhaps concerned over Ali's rise in popularity abroad or that he would avoid the draft by staying in Europe.[61]

On November 14, 1966, Ali stopped Cleveland Williams in the third round of their Houston, Texas, fight in what many boxing experts call Ali's greatest performance. Ali seemed virtually untouchable and able to score at will against his opponent, who was among the top contenders for the heavyweight title.

Then, the fight with Ernie Terrell was on again. On February 6, 1967, in Houston, Ali punished Terrell and won the match on a unanimous decision after the full fifteen rounds.

The fight was brutal. Ali seemed intent on making his opponent suffer. A win was not enough. Terrell had refused to call Ali by his Muslim name in the prefight publicity, and Ali was determined to make the challenger pay for it. "What's my name, Uncle Tom?" he shouted as he battered the outclassed Terrell.[62] That night against Terrell, Ali certainly did not act like the image most people had of conscientious objectors.

On March 22, 1967, Ali knocked out Zora Folley in the seventh round of their Madison Square Garden matchup. Though distracted by thoughts of his draft status, Ali had been in control of the bout from the beginning. Folley later had nothing but praise for his opponent: "There's just no way to train yourself for what he

Sacrifices

Basketball great Bill Russell, in an article he wrote for Sports Illustrated, *discussed at length the sacrifices Ali made by refusing to go into the armed forces. It was his most principled move, claimed Russell, and perhaps his most costly:*

"Ali is a stubborn man, and once he makes up his mind no one can change it. If you consider what he has given up for his beliefs, you can appreciate just how strong-minded he is. If he had wanted to compromise just a little, think of what he could have. All he would have to do is play down being a Black Muslim and accept the popular idea of what he should be.

It's tough for a man to be as devout as Ali. He could have said to himself, 'I want to be a so-called Negro leader, and I'll compromise in certain ways.' But if he did, he could not have lived with himself. Instead of that he has made far greater sacrifices than anyone seems to realize."

During weigh-in ceremonies Ali stares down his opponent, Ernie Terrell. Ali would win the bout on a unanimous decision after fifteen brutal rounds.

does: the moves, the speed, the punches and the way he changes style every time you think you got him figured. . . . Ali is something else."[63]

Draft Status Denied

In late 1966 Ali received his draft notice in the mail. It was not unexpected. His lawyers had been hard at work, but they had informed him that there was a strong chance the government would not accept his request for conscientious objector status.

It was not a great surprise to him when on March 6, 1967, the National Selective

Service Presidential Appeal Board voted against his request for conscientious objector status. The Nation of Islam was viewed as a political organization, not a religious one, so its members could not get an exemption—an argument that Ali and his lawyers would soon challenge. For now, Ali would remain classified as 1A.

He still maintained that he would refuse induction, no matter the penalty for it:

> I either have to obey the laws of the land or the laws of Allah, God. I'd rather die a Muslim. Six hundred million Muslims are with me to see if I am punished in this land of religious freedom. I have nothing to lose by standing up and following my own beliefs. I'll go down in history.[64]

In the early spring of 1967, as the date of his induction approached, Ali had the opportunity to change his mind. He and his lawyers met with lawyers from the Selective Service. It was suggested that if Ali would agree to induction, he would serve the country in a most useful fashion. He would not be sent to the front lines for fighting. He would serve as a morale booster, much like Joe Louis had, by making personal appearances and fighting exhibition matches. Reportedly, Ali was tempted by this opportunity. But he declined. He had come too far to turn back now.

Refusal and Punishment

On April 28, 1967, Muhammad Ali appeared before the draft board in Houston, Texas. He and about two dozen other young men entered the induction center and took several tests, then had lunch. Afterward they lined up in a room to be inducted into the armed forces. When asked to step forward, a gesture indicating the individual's consent, Ali did not move. He was motioned into another room, told of the severe consequences of such a refusal, then ushered back into the main room for another chance. Again, as his name was called, he refused to step forward.

The consequences for his refusal were swiftly handed out. On the same day the World Boxing Association stripped him of his title and the New York State Athletic Association revoked his license to box; soon, the nation's other state athletic associations would follow suit. Ali had not yet even been charged with a crime. Clearly, it was politics, not the law, that had taken away his championship and halted his career in boxing.

Some commentators had problems with the general treatment of Ali and especially the lightning response of the boxing commissions. Broadcaster Howard Cosell, a lawyer himself, was incensed:

> It was an outrage; an absolute disgrace. . . . Why? How could they? There'd been no grand jury impanelment, no arraignment. Due process of law hadn't even begun, yet they took away his livelihood because he failed the test of political and social conformity, and it took him seven years to get his title back. It's disgusting.[65]

(Cosell, for his consistent support of Ali and acceptance of Ali's Muslim name and identity, would thereafter be called the White Muslim by the angry public.)

However, in 1967 public commentators with opinions like Cosell's were few

Ali is escorted from the Armed Forces Examining and Entrance Station after refusing army induction, a move that would strip him of his title and boxing license.

Sports broadcaster Howard Cosell (pictured with Ali in 1981) was one of the few public commentators that spoke out in support of Ali and was willing to accept his Muslim name.

and far between. Journalists wrote that if Joe Louis and Jackie Robinson had served their country, then Muhammad Ali should be willing to go to war, too. He was a disgrace to his country. He was a traitor.

No Apologies

Ali himself voiced no regrets about his decision. He would not apologize to anyone. Following the dictates of his religion was more important than the opinion of those who condemned him. "Now it's over, and I've come through it," he later said in his autobiography. "I feel better than when I beat the eight-to-one odds and won the World Heavyweight Title from Liston."[66]

In the face of media and public uproar, he knew it was possible that he would never fight professionally again. That knowledge did not make him change his mind. Very few things could make Muhammad Ali change his mind once he made a decision.

What had Ali given up? Only the thing he had strived for his whole life— the heavyweight boxing championship of the world. He had given up the popularity that came with the title. He had given up the financial rewards that endorsements could bring him. More than that, he had given up the only livelihood he knew. He had given up everything he worked for and everything his great success could have brought him—for his public, principled, moral, unpopular stand, which had religious devotion at the heart of it, but which was also very personal.

About the strength of Ali's convictions, basketball great Bill Russell said,

If you consider what he has given up for his beliefs, you can appreciate just how strong-minded he is. If he had wanted to compromise just a little, think of what he could have. All he would have to do is play down being a Black Muslim and accept the popular idea of what he should be.[67]

Chapter

5 Exile and Return

On May 9, 1967, Muhammad Ali was indicted by a federal grand jury for refusing to submit to the draft. Three months later, on June 20, 1967, he was convicted. The maximum penalty for that conviction was a ten-thousand-dollar fine and up to five years in prison, and that's what the judge gave him. The State Department took away his passport so that he was unable to leave the country and escape prosecution—or fight in another country.

Ali's lawyers officially questioned the verdict of the jury, and in so doing began the process of appeal. (The conviction would, in fact, be upheld by a circuit court of appeals the following year, and then go on to the Supreme Court, where, in June 1971, it would be overturned.) Ali's lawyers also acted quickly to keep their client out of jail by posting a five-thousand-dollar bond.

While out of jail on bond and appealing his case, Ali should have been able to continue earning a living. With this in mind, Ali's promoters worked hard to get him a fight. They contacted as many state athletic commission officials as possible and tried to convince them to break the nationwide ban.

But their efforts were of no use. While some officials wanted the income and

Ali speaks to reporters after being convicted by a federal grand jury for refusing to submit to the draft.

A Pleasure

Angelo Dundee had been Muhammad Ali's trainer since Ali's second pro fight. During Ali's exile from boxing, Dundee was glad to be of help to Ali, in any way possible, as he acknowledges in Dave Anderson's book, In the Corner:

"If he was in Miami to give a talk at some college, he'd call me up and say, 'I want to come work at the gym. Do I have to pay dues?' I'd say, 'Muhammad, this is your gym.'

At the Fifth Street Gym, dues were twenty dollars a month. But not for him. This was his gym. He had his own little dressing room that was built before he won the title. When he wasn't around, nobody else used it. But when he'd come over to work out during his exile, if Jimmy Ellis was training, I'd have Muhammad spar with him. That way I'd be able to pay Muhammad just like I'd pay any other sparring partner, a hundred dollars a day. It was my pleasure. One time he was in Miami with his [second] wife, Belinda, and they were staying someplace that wasn't too nice. I made them go to the DuPont Plaza and I picked up the tab. It was my pleasure."

notoriety that a fight featuring Ali would give their state, no one wanted to go against the public opinion of the nation nor the wrath of angry political leaders or members of Congress, who had lambasted Ali for being a draft dodger. No state athletic commission in America was ready to grant Ali a license to fight. Thus began Muhammad Ali's exile from boxing.

Lectures

With no fight on the horizon to train for, Ali tended to other matters. At first he spent much of his time studying the teachings of Elijah Muhammad, attending meetings of the Nation of Islam, and traveling across the country to appear as a guest at mosques, Islamic houses of worship.

Having been cut off from his source of income, he went on the college lecture circuit. At first, he appeared to be stiff and uncomfortable speaking in front of college audiences. But as he gained more experience, and with hours of practice before hotel mirrors, his speeches became smooth and confident.

For the most part the college audiences—predominantly white and middle-class—responded positively. They listened respectfully to his explanations of Islam. They applauded his stand on individual liberty. They admired him for clearly having no political agenda and speaking only the truth of his heart. They laughed at his jokes and incessant kidding.

Exiled from boxing, Ali became a hit on the college lecture circuit. Here, he addresses Boston University students.

But they were dismayed by some of his views. In keeping with the drug-free message of the Nation of Islam, he complained about the smell of marijuana in the air. Seeing mixed couples in the audience, he would launch into a speech condemning interracial marriage—another view promoted by the Nation. He sounded strangely strict and old-fashioned to many in his audiences.

Nonetheless, those who heard Ali talk were inspired by him. How could one help but be influenced by a champion athlete at the top of his profession giving up so much—money, attention, prestige—because of his objection to a cause he believed to be wrong? His principled refusal to serve made others examine their own principles, and most were impressed by his arguments against participating in the war. Even those who opposed him admired his firm beliefs and his willingness to defend them.

Training had once consumed his time, but now he had room in his life to act as a husband and father. Shortly after his conviction, on August 17, 1967, he married Belinda Boyd, a seventeen-year-old member of the Nation of Islam from Chicago. They had been friends for a long time and were happy together as a young married couple. Within a year she gave birth to a daughter, Maryum. In 1970 Belinda gave birth to a set of twins, Jamillah and Rasheda. A boy, Muhammad Jr., was born in 1972.

America Changes

In 1967 Americans' opinions about the war in Vietnam had begun to change. As the war stretched on and on, Americans witnessed its maiming and destruction, brought to them in the daily newspapers and on the television news. The number

In 1967 Ali married a seventeen-year-old Nation of Islam member, Belinda Boyd. She is pictured here with the couple's four children.

of American forces in Vietnam had grown throughout the mid-1960s: 184,000 in 1965, 385,000 in 1966, and 485,000 in 1967. The death toll of Americans fighting in Vietnam rose, too: 1,369 dead in 1965, 5,008 in 1966, and 9,378 in 1967.[68] More and more Americans began to question American involvement. The "light at the end of the tunnel," which General William Westmoreland, commander of the U.S. forces in Vietnam, had been promising, was hardly visible.

Then came the Tet Offensive on January 20, 1968. The Tet Offensive was a surprise attack by the Vietcong on 116 cities and towns in South Vietnam during Tet, the Vietnamese new year holiday. The Vietcong made impressive advances, even to the point of attacking the American embassy compound in Saigon, before they were pushed back again. While gaining little territory, the Communist forces realized an inspiring victory in their aggressive push.

Americans were bewildered, frustrated, and angry. They knew full well that the light at the end of the tunnel was far dimmer than before, and that the end of the war was not in sight. Protests and mass demonstrations increased in frequency and size; they sometimes totalled hundreds of thousands of young people, who began to be joined by their parents, who resented, among other things, the increased taxes required to support the war effort. Some members of Congress attacked President Johnson's administration. Even the administration itself was divided by the issue of the war.

The year of 1968 was another turbulent one. The assassinations of Martin Luther King Jr., in April, and Robert Kennedy in June, were followed by urban riots: Chicago, Washington, Kansas City, Baltimore, and other cities burst into flames. In Vietnam over half a million American troops were stationed throughout the south of the country. By the end

U.S. Marines take cover behind a tank during the 1968 Tet Offensive. Following the surprise attack, American opposition to the war increased.

After a Reserve Officers' Training Corps building (center) was burned down, national guardsmen were sent to Kent State University to restore order. Confrontations between students and guardsmen resulted in the death of four unarmed antiwar demonstrators.

of the year, there were 14,592 American casualties.

Lies, Chaos, and Destruction

In 1968 the American public also learned that they had been lied to by the government. Back in July 1964 fighting broke out in the Gulf of Tonkin, off northern Vietnam. President Johnson, seeking congressional support for troop commitment, insisted that two American warships minding their own business in the Gulf had been savagely attacked by the Vietcong. Based on this argument, Johnson received his troops. But in 1968 Congress learned that the two American warships had been participating with the South Vietnamese in raids on North Vietnam when they were attacked.

The war continued dispensing chaos and destruction in southeast Asia and in America. In 1969 newly elected President Richard M. Nixon reduced American forces in Vietnam but increased the bombardment of North Vietnam, trying to put a quick end to the war. Also, for the first time, Vietcong supply lines in the neighboring countries of Cambodia and Laos were the focus of bombing by American forces. And in 1970 four unarmed students protesting the invasion of Cambodia by U.S. and South Vietnamese troops were killed in Ohio by national guardsmen at Kent State University.

Arguments that American radicals and leftists made years before now found a wide audience. One argument was that the war was a white man's war fought by black men; many more blacks than whites fought and died in the war. Another argument claimed that the war was fought against an underequipped peasant population; Americans witnessed the wholesale destruction of the Vietnam landscape and the dispersal of its poor urban and rural people.

As the decade came to a close, and in the wake of all these developments, Muhammad Ali's 1967 refusal to be inducted into the armed forces did not seem like such a crime anymore. He had merely been part of the tip of the iceberg of change, and now that the rest of the iceberg was exposed, the tip no longer looked all that threatening.

Public opinion toward him was more accepting. People felt that while the truth coming from the war got bent and bruised, the truth from Muhammad Ali had never changed. He began to be appreciated for speaking his mind—even by those who still disagreed with him. He was admired for standing by what he thought and felt and for suffering the consequences of his stand without complaint and without changing his story. He had principles. He had stuck to his guns. More and more the majority of Americans realized that, and they respected him.

Nation of Islam Ousts Ali

Another lesser known event occurred toward the end of Ali's exile: he was officially ousted for nearly a year from the Nation of Islam by Elijah Muhammad himself. When Ali joined the Nation, Elijah Muhammad had frowned upon Ali's profession, claiming it was a blood sport for the white man, who liked to see blacks fight each other. But he let Ali continue fighting, for this was the only livelihood Ali knew.

When Ali was exiled from boxing, Elijah Muhammad thought this good for the conscientious objector stand Ali had taken and for the help he could now do as a full-time minister of the Nation. But in 1969, when Ali publicly responded positively to the idea of fighting once again if the money was right, Elijah Muhammad was angry. He demanded that his adherents have complete faith in Allah to provide for

Ali (left) was exiled for nearly a year from the Nation of Islam by Elijah Muhammad (right), who denounced Ali for stating that he would return to boxing if the money was right.

them, and he denounced Ali for not having this faith.

Upon hearing of his ouster, Ali was truly hurt. He went to Elijah Muhammad and apologized. Herbert Muhammad finally pleaded Muhammad Ali's case to his father, and the rift between them was healed. By 1970 Ali was back in the Nation.

But 1970 marked the third year of his exile from boxing, and Ali was tired of being away. He had put on weight and looked a little flabby. Lawyers' expenses had mounted, as had his frustration at not being able to do anything about paying them. Regarding the future, he was resigned at one moment, hopeful the next. First he announced his retirement, then he announced he would try to return to the ring.

By the fall of 1970 Ali's promoters finally found a state willing to allow Ali to fight: Georgia. Georgia had no state boxing association, and two politicians—Atlanta mayor Sam Massell and state senator Leroy Johnson—helped put the fight together. Because Georgia governor Lester Maddox and several members of Congress objected to having Ali fight in Georgia—or anywhere—Ali first fought a test exhibition match in September. No one interceded, and plans were made for Ali to fight on October 26 against Jerry Quarry, a top heavyweight contender.

In the meantime, on September 28 a federal judge in New York State authorized the renewal of Ali's boxing license. Now Ali was again able to fight in Madison Square Garden. But a fight there would wait until he could show the world he was fit enough to be back in the ring against top fighters like Quarry.

Many thought Ali's fighting career was over. He had been out of boxing in what should have been the height of his career. It was hard to know how gracefully Ali had aged during his inactive years. One could not really tell from watching a boxer train;

Having Fun Before the Big Fight

Four weeks before his first fight with Joe Frazier, Muhammad Ali was training at the Fifth Street Gym in Miami. As Jose Torres remembers in his book Sting like a Bee: The Muhammad Ali Story, *Ali liked to have fun at the end of the day:*

"At seven we went in his limousine to pick up a friend at the airport. The show started.

Looking at one of the airport black employees, Ali yelled: 'Hey you! Do you think you can beat me? Come on.' And he pulled the guy toward him and began throwing punches over the head of the stranger. 'I'll beat you up so bad.' Then leaving the guy alone, Ali turned his head toward the crowd which began to form around him. 'I aaam the baaadest nigger in America,' he yelled. 'I'm going to play with Frazier and then I'm gonna come back here to beat . . . you,' he said, picking up a young black kid and then kissing him. 'You,' he continued, pointing to the same black kid, 'are probably the young man who will grow up to beat me. No one older than you can or could ever beat me. I am the greatest.'

Again, I was helplessly laughing. His remarks are funny no matter how many times he says them. 'You know who that man is laughing on the floor?' he asks. 'Hosey Torrays, the former light-heavyweight king. He is almost as pretty as me. Almost.'"

During Ali's exile from boxing, Joe Frazier (right) defeated Jimmy Ellis (left) for the world heavyweight championship.

the real test would come in the ring. Then everyone would see how much he had changed.

The boxing world had also changed without Ali. In his absence, a series of elimination matches were set up to decide a new world champion. Jimmy Ellis became the champion of the World Boxing Association and at about the same time Joe Frazier won the so-called New York World Heavyweight Championship. In a final match between the two on February 16, 1970, Frazier came away victorious. Ali had no feelings against Frazier, but he knew that Frazier was the one man between him and regaining his world championship.

The Great White Hope

But first Ali had to face Jerry Quarry. Quarry was billed as the Great White Hope, in reference to the white boxer

who sought to dethrone black champion Jack Johnson at the turn of the century.

Because the fight was set in the South, and because Ali was recognized as a champion of blacks, the Ali camp anticipated trouble during their stay in Georgia. And trouble came, first in the form of hate mail, then in the form of gunfire aimed at Ali's rural training camp and anonymous phone calls threatening even more violence should Ali continue to train in Georgia. Ali was undeterred, and he kept to his schedule. The threats died down and the camp was able to concentrate fully on their objective: to train their boxer to defeat Jerry Quarry.

The fight took place on October 26, 1970, and attendees stared at one another as much as at the fighters. Black money and power were strongly in evidence that evening. Jesse Jackson, Coretta Scott King, Sidney Poitier, Diana Ross, and Bill Cosby were among the black celebrities at the fight. Many in the audience proudly felt that Atlanta had become the South's new

Dr. Ralph Abernathy honors Ali after his comeback victory over Jerry Quarry.

capital of civil rights by virtue of accepting Ali's return to boxing.

The fight belonged to the former champion. Ali dominated the courageous Quarry from the beginning, and the fight was stopped in the third round because of cuts on Quarry's battered face. Victorious, Ali raised his hands and danced around the ring, as the crowd chanted his name.

Muhammad Ali was back.

Time Took Its Toll

In December Ali fought hard-hitting Oscar Bonavena in New York's Madison Square Garden. The fight went a full fifteen rounds before Ali defeated Bonavena by a fifteenth-round knockout. The former champion of the world clearly had trouble defeating a boxer whom, in his prime, he would have put away in the first few rounds.

A month shy of his twenty-ninth birthday, Ali's age was showing. While his hands were as quick as ever, his legs no longer sprinted him around the ring. Additionally, Ali discovered that he could take a lot of punishment, and this was more a curse than a blessing. In his earlier days no one quite knew if he could take a punch, since he was so quick that he was rarely hit hard by opponents; now he learned he could stand still and take punishment and continue fighting. Because he was no longer lightning quick on his feet, he was now hit by more punches than before.

Finally, the fight with Bonavena showed that Ali might no longer be capable of finishing an opponent quickly. It appeared that Ali was destined to spend more time in the ring absorbing more punishment.

Ali's bout with the hard-hitting Oscar Bonavena went a full fifteen rounds before Ali achieved victory with a knockout.

"A Terrible, Terrible Night"

Many who supported Ali and his stand against the war in Vietnam took personally Ali's loss to Joe Frazier in the fight in March 1971. In Thomas Hauser's Muhammad Ali: His Life and Times, *broadcaster Bryant Gumbel recalls why the loss affected him:*

"I felt as though everything I stood for had been beaten down and trampled. We'd all seen those pictures of the people with flags and hard hats beating up kids with long hair who were protesting, and this was our chance to get even in the ring. . . . And it was a terrible, terrible night. I'll never forget it as long as I live. The feeling was like when Richard Nixon won that crushing reelection mandate a year later. That was devastating, but Ali losing was much more personal because we had the feeling on the political side that our opinion was in the minority anyway. We knew we'd lose going in. It was almost like being part of the chosen ones; we were the only ones who had the whole world figured out, but the majority didn't see it our way. We knew the numbers weren't in our favor. That's why Ali-Frazier was so important, because that was the test. That was the level playing field; one against one, man against man. Now we'll show you bastards."

Ali had no time to dwell on the realities of the aging process, though. He had his sights set on the man who now held the title that had once been his. He needed to fight Joe Frazier for the championship.

Smokin' Joe

Joe Frazier was a relentless powerhouse of a fighter. Born on a farm in Beaufort, South Carolina, one of thirteen children, he had struggled all his life, moving forward relentlessly toward his goal of becoming the best fighter in the land,

regardless of any roadblocks or obstacles. And that is how he fought—plodding, relentless, indomitable. Frazier, called Smokin' Joe, was a powerful puncher, confident enough of his power to hurt that he would endure two or more punches from his opponent just to throw one crushing blow to the body or chin. Four inches shorter than the six-foot-three Ali, Frazier was "a brawler with the inexorable [relentless] power of a threshing machine."[69]

The Frazier-Ali match was what the fight world had been waiting for—two warriors, clearly the two best fighters in the world, battling for the championship. Negotiations were finalized, and Muhammad Ali, the challenger, and Joe Frazier,

(Left) Ali and Frazier engage in a shouting match during a contract-signing ceremony for their March 1971 fight.
(Below) Ali in training for the Frazier-Ali bout, which had become so highly anticipated it was referred to simply as "The Fight."

the champion, both undefeated in their professional careers, signed to meet in the ring at Madison Square Garden in New York in March of 1971. Each man would walk away with $2.5 million—an unprecedented sum. The fight had taken on such notoriety and importance that it was referred to simply as "The Fight."

A Vigorous Promotion

Frazier did not do much to promote the match. With Ali as a participant, he did not have to. It was not Frazier's style to open himself to the public the way Ali could. In the prefight publicity Frazier, defiant and headstrong, played second fiddle to Ali.

Ali's ring physician Ferdie Pacheco explains Frazier's role:

Joe Frazier never understood that he was part of the Act, that he was a co-

star, if a lesser one. For one fight, Joe Frazier became white, the public made him the good guy, the white guy, who was going to shut up the Black Muslim, draft-dodging, unpatriotic, loudmouth nigger, Muhammad Ali.[70]

Ali promoted the fight with wit and vigor. To the media, who awaited his words in the gym where he trained, Ali gave plenty of copy:

I'm the real Champion! I've been waiting for three years, listening to all this talk about who is the real Champ! . . . I told you he was a homemade Champion. I'm gonna have a good time for four or five rounds before I really get serious. I've been waiting for this.[71]

Walking down Broadway in New York City, crowds of people followed Ali as he scorned Frazier: "Where's Joe Frazier! Where's the White Folks' Champion! When I git him in the ring, you'll see. There'll be no contest."[72]

Ali did not hesitate to use strong language regarding Frazier. He called Frazier ugly. He declared that Joe Frazier was a stupid, ignorant man. He accused his opponent of being a lackey for the white man, while he, Ali, represented the black in the ghetto.

At first Frazier accepted Ali's insults as just a way to get people interested in the fight. But as the insults grew harsher, so did Frazier's opinion of Ali. Frazier came to genuinely hate Ali. The people who worked around Frazier could not help but notice the dedication, persistence, and anger with which the champion trained for his upcoming meeting in the ring with the man who had nasty things to say about him. One member of Frazier's camp said of Ali: "No one has ever worked so hard on the buildup for his own funeral."[73]

The Fight

The fight took place on March 8, 1971. A sellout crowd was in attendance. In fact, tickets had been sold out a month in advance of the fight. The interest in this fight was phenomenal. The fight was carried on closed circuit television in movie theaters throughout the United States. It was, in fact, a worldwide media event, made so by technology advanced enough to carry it to all corners of the earth.

In his autobiography Ali recalled the moment he realized how tough an opponent Joe Frazier was going to be. Ali climbed into the ring and began warming up, circling around the canvas.

Accidentally on purpose, I touch Frazier's shoulders as he stands in his corner. For a split second we look at each other, eye to eye. I'm shaken, and when the bell rings I fight two fights: the fight that was in my mind—the fight I talked about—and the one I am in for fifteen rounds. And they are not exactly the same.[74]

In the early part of the match each fighter displayed moments of brilliance and courage. Frazier, in his constant, plodding attack, would be momentarily jolted by an Ali punch, but a faint grin would appear on his battered, puffy face as he gathered himself, punched his gloves together in front of him, and continued his pursuit of the former champ. Ali responded by dancing away and jabbing Frazier's face at will, pounding him with hooks and uppercuts.

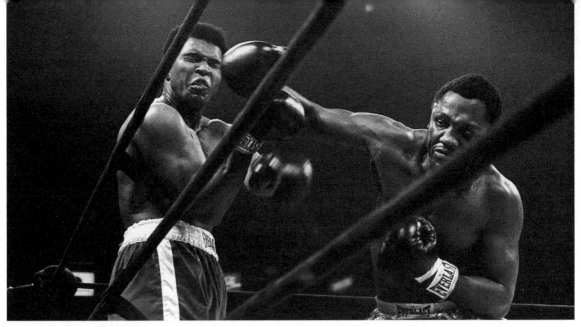

Frazier connects solidly with a long right to Ali's face. The two took turns dominating one another until the fifteenth round, when Ali became a stationary target for the relentless Frazier.

The first few rounds went to Ali, the next few to Frazier. Through the ninth round the two fighters took turns dominating one another. In the tenth round Frazier was the master, and he punished the weary Ali in that round and the next. The twelfth and thirteenth rounds were Frazier's, too. Ali came back to life in the fourteenth, dancing beautifully, scoring at will; however, in the fifteenth round, Ali's legs would dance for him no longer.

A Courageous Fight, A Dignified Loss

Now Ali was nearly a stationary target, and Frazier's booming left hook found its mark early in the round. Ali was caught with a tremendous blow, flush on the chin. He went down, his legs flying up and pointing to the ring lights. It was a fight-stopping blow, an injurious blow, a blow from which Ali should have stayed on the canvas to recover. But courageously, Ali hurried to his feet and went straight at Frazier, holding him now, staying close, tying up his arms, for the duration of the round. "He took the best punch of any heavyweight I ever saw, a tremendous left hook," recalled trainer Angelo Dundee. "When he got up as fast as anybody could get up, I never was prouder of him." [75] Then the fight was over. The referee and judges awarded a close but unanimous decision to the champion, Joe Frazier.

Many took the loss very personally. Those sympathetic to Ali's principled stand against the Vietnam War years before and who had revered him as a hero for standing up against the establishment now felt especially pained. Television broadcaster Bryant Gumbel remembers his feelings the night Ali tried to win back his championship but failed:

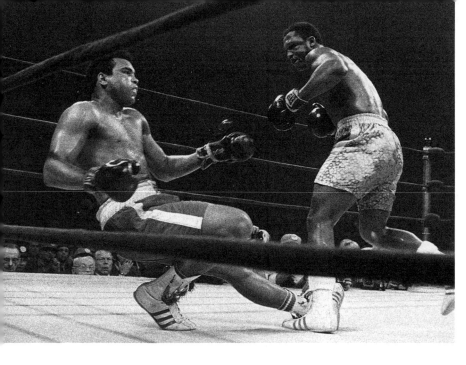

Ali is knocked to the canvas by a vicious left hook from Frazier, who became the undisputed heavyweight champion after a close but unanimous fifteen-round decision.

I felt as though everything I stood for had been beaten down and trampled. We'd all seen those pictures of the people with flags and hard hats beating up kids with long hair who were protesting, and this was our chance to get even in the ring. . . . And it was a terrible, terrible night. I'll never forget it as long as I live.[76]

Ali's response was nothing less than gracious and dignified. It had not been a terrible night for him. He was not devastated. The day after the fight he consoled many of the reporters who came to interview him. He told them that his losing was not so important, that there were other worse events in the world, such as plane crashes and assassinations. Life went on, he said, and you had to put your losses behind you.

As Robert Lipsyte remembers, a reporter interrupted Ali: "'Champ. . . .'

"'Don't call me the champ,' said Ali gently, 'Joe's the champ now.'"[77]

Ali put his loss further in perspective:

We all have to take defeats in life. We lose loved ones, or a man loses his property or his job. All kinds of things set us back, but life goes on. . . . Soon this will be old news. People got lives to lead, bills to pay, mouths to feed. Maybe a plane will go down with ninety persons in it. Or a great man will be assassinated. That will be more important than Ali losing. I never wanted to lose, never thought I would, but the thing that matters is how you lose. I'm not crying. My friends should not cry.[78]

Muhammad Ali was right in insisting that no one cry about his loss. After all, there had been so much he had won. With his principled refusal to submit to the draft, he had won the appreciation and respect of many. With his patience and determination, he had won the resumption of his boxing career. With his indomitable spirit, he had won back his place in the public eye. The Greatest was back.

Chapter

6 Winning Back the Title

On June 28, 1971, Ali won a victory outside the ring. On that day the Supreme Court reversed his 1967 conviction for refusing induction to the military. Further, the Supreme Court accused the Justice Department of providing misleading evidence concerning Ali's conscientious objector claim. Indeed, the Supreme Court insisted, Ali's claim to moral and religious principles was valid and sincere and should have been treated that way—like that of any other conscientious objector. He should not have been drafted in the first place. Ali had little to say about the Supreme Court's ruling. He had already made his return to the ring and the whole world had been witness to it; he had already been vindicated.

But he still hungered for the heavyweight title, and he did not know when he would get a crack at it again. Angry over Ali's incessant insults before the last fight, Frazier was now pleased to be in the position to stand back and let the other fighter do the work. He had what Ali wanted—the heavyweight championship. Ali would have to earn another chance to win it all over again, by beating other top title contenders.

His sights set on fighting Frazier again, Ali met all challengers in his march to-

Ali compares fists with boyhood friend Jimmy Ellis, who he fought and defeated during his march toward earning another chance to fight for the title.

ward another opportunity to fight for the title. On July 26, 1971, he fought and defeated his boyhood friend, Jimmy Ellis, in the twelfth round of their fight in Houston. He beat Buster Mathis in Houston, then traveled to Switzerland to defeat Jurgen Blin in Zurich on December 26. He met Mac Foster, George Chuvalo, Jerry Quarry, then faced Al Lewis, Floyd Patterson, and finally, Bob Foster. Ali was victorious in each fight.

Then Ali's plan to fight Joe Frazier for the title changed. On January 22, 1973, in Kingston, Jamaica, Joe Frazier lost the heavyweight crown to Olympic gold medalist George Foreman in the second round of their fight. The awesome Foreman had demolished Frazier, sending the champion literally up off the canvas with a thunderous uppercut.

With his focus now on George Foreman, Ali signed for a couple of fights that his manager, Herbert Muhammad, thought would be relatively easy. First, Ali met and handily defeated Joe Bugner, an Englishman, in Las Vegas. Then came a relative unknown named Ken Norton. They met in San Diego on March 31, 1973. In the ring, Norton would prove to be quite a surprise.

A Broken Jaw

In the first round of the fight, Norton, a former marine and a powerful puncher with an awkward style, broke Ali's jaw. Angelo Dundee remembered when Ali came back to the corner after the injury: "I no-

With his sights set on fighting new heavyweight champion George Foreman, Ali handily defeats Englishman Joe Bugner (pictured).

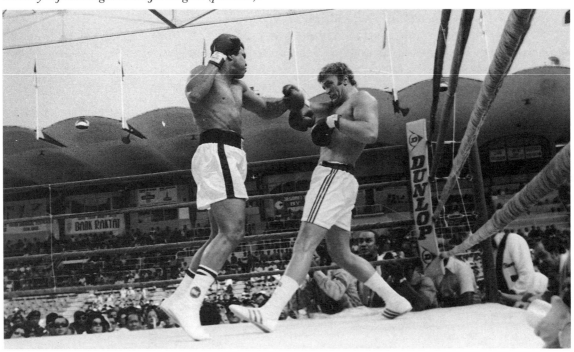

Opposing Images

In his book Beyond the Ring: The Role of Boxing in American Society, *author Jeffrey T. Sammons discusses the contrasting images of challenger Muhammad Ali and champion George Foreman, who would meet for the heavyweight championship in Zaire:*

"Although Ali's legal battles were behind him, he still stimulated controversy wherever he went, whatever he did. He remained the 'black menace' of his time, and in the absence of bona fide [authentic] 'white hopes,' other black boxers were still expected to humble him. . . . At the [1968] Olympic Games in Mexico City, Foreman had walked around the ring waving a tiny American flag to celebrate his gold medal victory—quite a contrast to Tommie Smith and John Carlos, the track stars who stood on the winners' stand with clenched fists in protest of racial injustice. Foreman capitalized on the incident in 'Don't Knock the American System to Me,' a patriotic message that found currency with the boxing crowd and with politicians of various persuasions who jumped at the chance to justify their own ideologies [beliefs] and further their own programs. With the assistance of a ghost [anonymous] author, Foreman wrote: 'There were more than 2,000 black athletes in those Olympic Games in all sports. I was afraid—even with the USA on my jersey—they might not know I was an American. And I wanted everybody to know, and to know that at that moment, I was one of the happiest Americans who ever lived. So, I took the little American flag from the pocket of my robe and waved it as I took a bow to each of the ring's four corners.'"

George Foreman proudly waves an American flag after winning a gold medal in the 1968 Olympics.

After suffering defeat and a broken jaw in their first bout, Ali threatens Ken Norton at a contract-signing ceremony for their rematch.

ticed the dark blood in his mouth. I told him, 'I think your jaw's busted. I think I'm going to have to stop this fight.' He said, 'Don't you stop it. I'll beat this bum. Don't you stop it.'"[79]

Dundee heeded the request. Ali came out of his corner for the second round and began to fight defensively, protecting his face. He tried to fend off Norton this way for the rest of the fight, which went a full twelve rounds. Ali, unable to mount an effective attack, lost by decision.

The fact that Ali fought for twelve rounds with a broken jaw impressed many people. Those critics who had questioned Ali's ability to take a punch were silenced; they had new respect for him. Angelo Dundee, like most observers, thought Ali's refusal to let the fight be stopped was an act of great spirit and valor: "Going twelve rounds with that busted jaw, Muhammad had so much courage. . . . When we got to the hospital, he's consoling me. I felt so bad, I was practically crying. But he's saying, 'Don't worry, we'll be back.'"[80]

Ali gave credit where credit was due. After having his jaw set and wired, Ali spoke to the media: "Norton beat me today. Fair and square. I tried to win, but he was too tough today. Tomorrow, when I get well, I'll go out and whup his ass, but today, Norton was the better man."[81]

Ali got the opportunity to make good on his word. He and Norton met in a rematch on September 10 in Los Angeles. The fight was close, for again Ali had trouble with Norton's relentless, awkward style. But Ali won the decision in twelve rounds. It was another vindication of his ability to win back the championship.

After disposing of Rudi Lubbers just six weeks after the second Norton fight, on January 28, 1974, Ali's next opponent was Joe Frazier. They met at Madison Square Garden, the site of their first bout. Ali seemed more nimble in this bout and proved to be a hard target for Frazier to find. Ali's dancing and jabbing frustrated Frazier, and though Ali did not knock Frazier down, he did win a unanimous decision.

Ali, now thirty-two, had once again rightfully earned a shot at the title, now held by twenty-five-year-old George Foreman. A former Olympic gold medalist from the 1968 Mexico City games, Foreman was a giant of a man and a devastating puncher, with a record of 40-0, including thirty-seven knockouts.

Foreman was also a black champion acceptable to white society. In the Mexico City games after his final victory, he had paraded around the boxing ring, waving a small American flag to the cheering crowd. American politicians recognized his patriotism and congratulated him and praised him as the kind of hero American youngsters needed to emulate. Foreman's image as a patriot was quite at odds with Ali's image of dogged individualism.

The Rumble in the Jungle

Ali signed to fight George Foreman for an unprecedented five million dollars. The fight would be on September 25, 1974, in Kinshasa, Zaire, formerly the Belgian Congo. This part of the world, now free and considered a developing nation, had been the site of the worst ravages of both colonialism and the slave trade for several centuries. Promoter Don King happily boasted to the media that this fight was a black-only fight: it was fought by blacks before a black audience in a black country in Africa, a black continent. And the whole world, King claimed, would be watching.

Ali was excited about the fight, which he called the Rumble in the Jungle. Be-

President Joseph Mobutu (center) introduces Ali and Foreman to the people of Zaire before their "Rumble in the Jungle."

fore Ali, and with few exceptions, the heavyweight championship had always been contested on American soil. But Ali had brought championship boxing to the world both early in his career and now, during his comeback.

A Strategy to Win

Ali trained hard, as usual, but more important than his physical training was his study of Foreman's style and his efforts to come up with a strategy to combat it. He had advisers and spies who brought him facts and insights about Foreman's strengths and weaknesses. Ali learned, for instance, that he must not bend down in the fight, for Foreman had a tremendous uppercut. One of them had lifted Joe Frazier off the canvas in their title fight months before. To win, Ali decided, he must keep moving out of range of Foreman's arcing punches. He must keep changing direction, so that the less-agile Foreman would waste energy changing direction and grow frustrated and tired and maybe leave himself open to Ali. Ali also knew that Foreman had never gone more than three rounds in a championship fight, and he decided he must make the fight last into the later rounds, because this was unfamiliar territory for Foreman. Ali was optimistic about his ability to defeat Foreman. He just had to stick to his strategy.

Boxing critics were not as optimistic about Ali's chances. In fact, most gave him no chance of winning. Many feared that he would be badly injured. As the day of the fight approached, even his own camp was solemn.

Suddenly, important news issued from the Foreman camp: Foreman had been cut over the eye in a sparring session, and the fight had to be postponed. Ali was upset at first. He wanted to stay on his schedule. But he soon relaxed, realizing that the delay would give him more time to prepare himself to win back the championship.

A Spy's Report

Ali paid spies to reveal Foreman's training regimen, his strengths, and his weaknesses. One spy was Bossman Jones. In his autobiography, The Greatest: My Own Story, *Ali remembers Jones's revelations:*

"The people accept George as a brute and they come to see him knock somebody out. George got the guns to do it. I see fighters who could stun you, who could knock you out, but George is the first one I been in the ring with I know can kill you. He may never kill nobody and I hope he never does, but he's got the power to kill, and he knows it. He has a special punch called the 'anywhere' punch because anywhere it hits you, it breaks something inside you—a muscle, a bone, shoulder, a finger, a rib."

After attempting to unsettle Foreman with taunts before the fight began, Ali readies for a left jab in the first round of their bout.

The Fight

On October 30 at four o'clock in the morning in Zaire—ten o'clock in the evening of the previous day in New York— Ali entered the ring at the center of a renovated soccer stadium. The ring was covered in case of rain, and flooded with light. The stands were filled with cheering, chanting Zairians.

Foreman was late getting to the ring, and Ali, always looking for an edge, used this time to his advantage. He walked around the ring, getting used to it. He tested the tension of the ring ropes and felt glad that he had this opportunity to make himself at home in the ring. "Instead of starting out cold, I will know more about the atmosphere than my opponent," he reflected.[82] Finally, ten minutes after Ali's entrance, Foreman climbed into the ring.

Ali met Foreman at the middle of the ring for the standard referee's instructions, where he continued to seek an ad-

vantage. In his autobiography Ali recalls his own efforts to unsettle Foreman just before their fight began:

> "You're gonna get yourself beat tonight in front of all these Africans."
>
> The referee's head jerks up. "Ali, no talking! Listen to the instructions." He goes on. "No hitting below the belt, no kidney punches. . . ."
>
> "Never mind that stuff, sucker." I speak low. "I'm gonna hit you everywhere but under the bottom of your big funky feet, Chump! You got to go, sucker!"
>
> "Ali, I warned you," the referee snaps. "Be quiet!"[83]

Ali continued his threats until the referee finally dismissed both men to their corners. Ali turned east, toward Mecca, the holiest site of the Islam religion, and said a short prayer, then waited for the bell. In the background, he could hear the fans chanting: "Ali, bomaye"—*Ali, kill him.*

At the bell Ali rushed out and threw a dangerous right cross to the top of

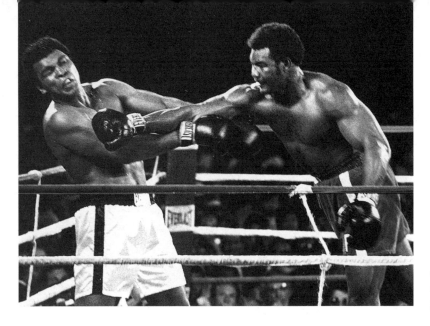

Ali suffers the impact of one of Foreman's enormously powerful punches.

Foreman's head, to surprise him. Several moments later, though, Ali realized that everything he had heard about Foreman's enormous power was true, as the champion bullied him against the ropes and began punching. While Bundini screamed for Ali to dance away from the attack, Ali caught some terrible shots from Foreman, who threw right-handed and left-handed looping hooks that he called "anywhere punches": they did damage anywhere they landed.

Rope-a-Dope

In the second round, too, Ali found he could not get away from Foreman, who had been trained to move to the right or left as Ali moved, thereby cutting off Ali's escape routes. Ali found himself trapped. Then and there Ali changed his strategy. He decided to stay on the ropes and absorb Foreman's punches until the other man was too tired to throw them with

power—a strategy he would later dub the "rope-a-dope." It was a gamble, but Ali thought he would tire himself out if he tried to keep away from Foreman, who took three steps to Ali's six.

Surprised and pleased to see his opponent standing there in front of him, a stationary target, Foreman landed tremendous blows on Ali's arms and shoulders. The people in Ali's corner were horrified. They screamed for Ali to get away, to get off the ropes. But Ali stayed put, absorbing the storm of punches thrown by the determined champion, sometimes being jarred by one, protecting his head and body as well as he could.

Ali stayed on the ropes in the third round, too, and this time he was nearly knocked out. He would later recall Foreman's blows and the warning cries from his own corner:

George is throwing bombs at my head. I lean back, but he stays on top of me. I'm amazed at how he can pack power into every punch. Every punch is a haymaker [powerful blow]. I block them from my head, and suddenly he switches, comes up from the floor with an uppercut that seems to blow my jaw off. I'm hurt. I try to hold on.

"GET OFF THE ROPES! DANCE, CHAMP, DANCE!"

I try to move off, but he punches me back like a rag doll. . . . I've got to hold on. I've got to keep him from following up. George senses that I'm hurt, and he's coming in for the kill. I block, move back and weave. It's the longest round I've ever fought in my life, but near the end my head begins to clear.[84]

Ali continued his strategy of lying back on the ropes, absorbing Foreman's thundering blows. But little by little, here and again through the middle rounds of the fight, he took his own shots at Foreman. His counterattacks came suddenly, without warning, and near the end of each round—to surprise Foreman but also to leave a favorable impression with the judges at ringside, who scored each round immediately after it finished. Foreman grew befuddled—how could this old man of thirty-two take such powerful blows and still have snap in his punches? Ali, studying Foreman's eyes, was encouraged to see the champion losing confidence.

Just as Ali had planned, Foreman slowed down. By the seventh round the champion had expended a lot of energy throwing punches. He had not yet gained his second wind and he gasped for breath. Ali took advantage of the situation and tried to talk Foreman's confidence away. He grabbed Foreman and held him, and as the referee came to break the two fighters apart, Ali began his taunt: "You got eight more rounds to go, sucker! Eight more rounds, and look how tired you are. I ain't even got started, and you out of breath! Look at you! Out of gas, and I'm whippin' you."[85]

Ali Takes Control

In round eight, Ali took control. He waited for his opening, then took it. He landed three sharp right-handed crosses to Foreman's head, then came back with a left, and then with what writer Robert Lipsyte called "the Bomb, a right-hand sledgehammer" to the jaw.[86]

After absorbing a tremendous flurry of blows, Ali takes control in the eighth round, dominating a now wearied Foreman.

A victorious Ali raises his gloves in triumph after regaining the world heavyweight championship.

Ali watched Foreman circle, stunned, then fall slowly, finally crashing in a heap to the canvas. He watched as the referee raised his arm for the count ten times. After the tenth, Foreman was up on his feet. But the fight was over. The crowd cheered wildly. Fans and reporters poured into the ring. The referee grabbed and lifted the new champ's arm to signal victory. Muhammad Ali had regained the heavyweight championship of the world.

In the dressing room after the fight, though exhausted, Ali could not keep from bragging about his accomplishment. Full of scorn for the reporters who had given him little chance to win the fight, he held court in typical Muhammad Ali style:

> I told you all I would do it, but did you listen? He was scared, he was humiliated. I told you I was the greatest heavyweight of all time. I didn't dance. I wanted him to tire, to lose power. I decided to use the ropes. He punched like a sissy.[87]

Later, he had kinder words for Foreman. In his autobiography Ali paid measured homage to the young champion he had dethroned that early morning in Africa: "I take nothing away from George. He can still beat any man in the world. Except me."[88]

7 Too Long in the Ring

Before his exile Muhammad Ali had been so quick as a defensive fighter that few opponents' blows found their mark. His face remained unblemished, his hips and ribs unbruised. Since his comeback, though, he had slowed down. He was struck by many blows he once would have avoided easily.

The Foreman bout took a lot out of Ali. Ali's strategy had worked like a charm: staying on the ropes and absorbing Foreman's punches had tired Foreman and ultimately made him a target for Ali's flurry of knockout punches. But Ali's body, on the receiving end of so many Foreman punches, was a mess. His arms were terribly bruised. His ribs ached. More importantly, he had taken a number of Foreman's heaviest blows to the head. After the Foreman bout, the Greatest certainly was not the Healthiest, and his health was soon to become a problem.

But a different kind of problem presented itself a few months after Ali's fight with Foreman. Elijah Muhammad, prophet and spiritual leader of the Nation of Islam, died on February 25, 1975. With the death of the man who called whites "the Devil race," many in the Nation of Islam waited to see the direction the new leadership would take. Headed by one of Elijah

Herbert Muhammad (center), son of Nation of Islam prophet Elijah, took over as Ali's manager in 1966. Ali's alliance with the Nation of Islam was strengthened following the death of Elijah, when the new leadership began to stress racial harmony instead of hatred toward whites.

"That's a Dirty Man"

Joe Frazier took offense at many of the things Ali said about him while promoting their fights. Writing in Sports Illustrated, *Mark Kram records his own meeting with Frazier just before the Thrilla in Manila:*

"Over and over Ali shouts 'Joe Frazier is a gorilla, and he's gonna fall in Manila.' The gorilla label, with all its inherent racism, stings. Frazier glances at a picture on his dresser. 'Look at my beautiful kids,' he says, plaintively. 'Now, how can I be a gorilla? That's a dirty man. He's just like a kid when you play with him. He don't wanna stop, and then ya gots to whup him to make him behave. That's what this jerk Clay [Ali] is like. Well, I guess he gonna talk. Ain't no way to stop him, but there will come that moment when he gonna be all alone, when he gonna hear that knock on the door, gonna hear it's time to go to the ring, and then he's gonna remember what it's like to be in with me, how hard and long this night's gonna be.'"

Muhammad's sons, Wallace Muhammad, would the Nation still proclaim that all whites were devils? Or would there be a moderation of their long-held views?

Soon it was clear that the Nation of Islam under Wallace Muhammad stressed traditional Islam and racial harmony. Ali was relieved. He would have found it hard to reaffirm the Nation's former belief that white people were devils. He had had many positive experiences with white people. He had been treated well by white lawyers, promoters, and friends.

In his book *Muhammad Ali: His Life and Times*, author Thomas Hauser records Ali describing his changing views after Elijah Muhammad died:

I don't hate whites. That was history, but it's coming to an end. We're in a new phase, a resurrection. Elijah taught us to be independent, to clean ourselves up, to be proud and healthy. He stressed the bad things the white man did to us so we could get free and strong. Now, his son Wallace is showing us there are good and bad regardless of color, that the devil is in the mind and heart, not the skin. We Muslims hate injustice and evil, but we don't have time to hate people. White people wouldn't be here if God didn't mean them to be.[89]

At peace with his religious beliefs, Ali was troubled by something left undone in his professional career: he and Joe Frazier had fought twice and each had won once. Who was the superior fighter?

One more fight was in order between Ali, now thirty-three years old, and Joe Frazier, thirty-one. The fans wanted to see it and the combatants were eager to engage each other. Ali tuned up for his showdown with Frazier by defeating Chuck Wepner, Ron Lyle, and then, for the second time, Joe Bugner. The Thrilla in Manila, Ali's third fight with Joe Frazier, was set to take place in the Philippine Coliseum, just outside of Manila, the Philippines, on October 1, 1975.

The Thrilla in Manila

As with the Rumble in the Jungle, the Thrilla in Manila, as Ali called his upcoming third fight with Frazier, would be held in a developing third world nation. Philippine president Ferdinand Marcos and his wife Imelda treated Ali and Frazier warmly. The Marcoses knew that the fight would put the Philippines in the spotlight of the world. The fighters had numerous public relations responsibilities as they prepared to battle one another for the third time. Ali, displaying his usual bravado and blus-

ter, excited local crowds with his scorn and condemnation of his opponent. As always, the media was delighted to report each new insult that Ali came up with.

Joe Frazier once again took offense at things Ali said about him. It seemed to Frazier that Ali went too far. Promoting a fight was one thing, but Frazier felt that Ali stepped beyond the usual limits of promotion and into the arena of personal insult. Writer Mark Kram recalls:

Over and over Ali shouts "Joe Frazier is a gorilla, and he's gonna fall in Manila." The gorilla label, with all its inherent racism, stings. Frazier glances at a picture on his dresser. "Look at my beautiful kids," he says, plaintively. "Now, how can I be a gorilla? That's a dirty man. He's just like a kid when you play with him. He don't wanna stop, and then ya gots to whup him to make him behave. That's what this jerk Clay [Ali] is like."[90]

Ali rises from the canvas after being knocked down by Chuck Wepner in the ninth round of their 1975 bout. Sylvester Stallone would later create his Rocky character after watching Wepner's heroic fight against Ali.

While preparing in the Philippines for his third fight with Frazier, Ali was accompanied by Veronica Porsche (right), who later became his third wife.

Before their third fight, Joe Frazier was not the only one with a personal gripe against Ali. The champion had brought his girlfriend, Veronica Porsche—who would become his third wife—to Manila and made the mistake of allowing her to be identified by President Marcos and the press as Ali's wife. When this story reached the newspapers in the United States, an angry Belinda Ali boarded a plane and flew to Manila to have it out with her husband. In the privacy of Ali's hotel room, husband and wife traded accusations and oaths and tossed around the furniture. Then, just as quickly as she had arrived, Belinda left the hotel and flew back to the United States. Shortly afterward, they legally ended their marriage.

Torture in the Ring

Marital tensions appeared not to have affected Ali's ring performance, and the world was treated to one of the greatest fights in the history of boxing. The early rounds belonged to Ali, the middle rounds to Frazier, and when in the twelfth round it looked like Frazier would go on to defeat Ali, the champion reached for a reserve of energy and took the fight back from the relentless Frazier. In the thirteenth round Frazier's mouthpiece shot out into the crowd after an Ali blow. By the middle of the fourteenth round, it was clear that both men had absorbed more punishment than ever before in any single fight. Author John Hennessey describes the action:

> Frazier, arms by his side and his head resembling a football, took punch after punch but just refused to stop march-

Ali retained his heavyweight title in a brutal fourteen-round bout with Frazier, in which both fighters absorbed terrible punishment.

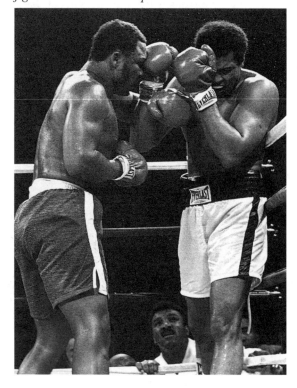

ing forward. Ali, at melting point but disguising it brilliantly, threw everything in his bid to end the torture.[91]

Earlier, Ali had described the types of punches he would use to defeat Frazier: "I got a balloon punch and a needle punch. The balloon punch is a left jab, which swells him up, blows him up, puffs him up. And the needle's gonna bust him. That's the right hand. Whop!"[92]

Both fighters were injured, and the torture ended at the conclusion of the fourteenth round. Frazier was unable to come out of the fifteenth round, giving Ali the victory. As the referee terminated the bout, Ali's legs gave out and he fell to the canvas.

After the fight it was obvious that both fighters had absorbed terrible punish-ment. Frazier's face was a mass of welts, and both eyes were nearly swollen shut. Ali, too, was covered with welts, and his hips were discolored from the bombs Frazier threw. He later insisted that this experience was the closest thing to death that he had ever experienced.

Even with all the pain he suffered at Joe Frazier's hands, at this point in his career Ali did not seriously consider retiring. He enjoyed the position he was in too much to give it up. Ali's physician Ferdie Pacheco recalls that Ali talked of retiring

for about thirty seconds. . . . Like a fading movie star milking an audience, he would throw out the thought, then lay back and await the sweet sound of his public yelling at him:

Quick Thinking

In 1976 Ali appeared on the CBS news show Face the Nation, *a forum usually reserved for national politicians and heads of state. Jeffrey T. Sammons, in his book* Beyond the Ring: The Role of Boxing in America Society, *recalls Ali's quick thinking in the face of a potentially embarrassing question:*

"When some of the questions betrayed lingering doubts about his religious convictions and sincerity, Ali's answers clearly revealed a mind that worked as fast as his hands and feet, one that had long kept the press off-guard. Fred Graham, legal correspondent for CBS, and Ali engaged in a classic exchange:

GRAHAM: Well, you have a reputation as—you're separated from your wife, and you have a reputation as a man who has a sharp eye for the ladies. Now, how is that going to be consistent with your role as a religious leader in the years ahead?

ALI: Well, as far as my personal beliefs are concerned I don't talk about them in public; as far as my personal problems with family, these are things I don't discuss in public, especially on high-class shows like I was told yours would be, so I don't even expect to talk about that here."

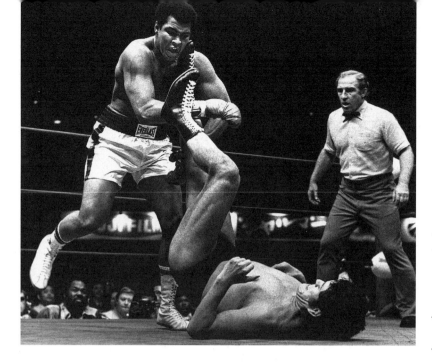

Professional wrestler Antonio Inoki insisted on taking his match with Ali for "the martial arts championship of the world" seriously. Set up for entertainment, the fight turned into an embarrassment for Ali.

'No! No! Champ, you're too young! You got years left ahead of you.' [93]

Ali felt he was still in shape for fighting and would not consider giving up the title and the attention—and the money. He had financial responsibilities to consider, of course. Members of his entourage had to make a living, and they encouraged him to keep fighting. The Nation of Islam also played a role in his decision to continue fighting. According to Ferdie Pacheco, Herbert Muhammad and the men managing Ali "assured me he would only have easy fights from now on, pick up major bucks, not risk his health, and coast to retirement." [94]

Mostly, though, he loved being in the spotlight and having the press hanging on his every word. Had he wanted to call it quits, he surely would have. Ali was always stubborn and always insisted on making his own decisions, regardless of what might come of them. He was not ready to give up being heavyweight champion of the world.

Mere Skirmishes

Having fought major battles nearly back-to-back with Foreman and then Frazier, Ali settled for mere skirmishes now, with opponents of less than formidable ability. Ali scored dull victories over Belgian champ Jean-Pierre Coopman, journeyman heavyweight Jimmy Young, and England's Richard Dunn.

In Tokyo, Japan, on June 26, 1976, Ali engaged in an embarrassing match against professional wrestler Antonio Inoki for "the martial arts championship of the world." The plan for the fight—really an entertainment—was for Ali to win the decision after a theatrical brawl, then fall victim to a sneak attack by the enraged Inoki. It seemed like an easy payday for both men and their camps. Everyone involved agreed to the scenario ahead of time—except Inoki, who insisted on taking the fight seriously. As it turned out, Ali and the wrestler were in the ring for fifteen boring rounds, during which time Ali threw five or six punches while the careful wrestler stayed close to the mat, kicking at Ali's calves and thighs. Ali won the decision but had to be hospitalized later to keep the blood clots in his bruised legs from spreading through his body.

Ali then fought Ken Norton for the third time. They battled for fifteen tough rounds in New York's Yankee Stadium, and Ali barely won the decision. In fact, many in the stands that night thought Norton would have won the decision had he not slacked off in the last round in accordance with instructions from his cornermen. They were confident of his performance thus far and wanted him to coast to victory with little risk. Ali had been visibly tired and his timing was off, but again he had won.

Once it had been Ali's code not to get hit during a fight; now his legs no longer carried him from harm's way. On May 16, 1977, against lackluster Alfredo Evange-lista of Spain, Ali went the distance—fifteen rounds—for the decision.

Distractions

In 1977 there were other things on Ali's mind besides boxing. He divorced Belinda and married Veronica Porsche; the couple already had a nine-month-old child. Now Ali had two former wives to support, as well as four children from his marriage with Belinda, and a third wife and a new baby, Hana. Also, his autobiography was published and an autobiographical movie, *The Greatest*, was released. The works had unrealistically positive, storybook presentations and invited questions about their truthfulness. Ali had little interest in the autobiography, written with the aid of writer Richard Durham, and in fact read it completely only after it had been published; the movie was clearly fictionalized.

Artist Andy Warhol photographs Ali with his daughter Hana and wife Veronica.

At this time the most obvious truth was that Ali should quit boxing. He was absorbing far too much punishment, not only during each prize fight but also on a daily basis while in training. Says his physician, Ferdie Pacheco:

> If I had to pick a spot to tell him, "You've got all your marbles, but don't go on anymore," no question, it would have been after Frazier. That's when it really started to fall apart. He began to take beatings, not just in fights but in the gym. Even sparring, he'd do the rope-a-dope because he couldn't avoid punches the way he did when he was young. And I don't care how good you are at rope-a-doping. If you block ninety-five punches out of a hundred, the other five are getting in.[95]

Those five-out-of-a-hundred punches, plus the punches he absorbed during matches, contributed to Ali's physical decline. After defeating hard-hitting Earnie Shavers on September 29, 1977, Ali received bad news from a lab report: his kidneys were deteriorating. They were letting pure blood through instead of filtering out the wastes to produce urine. In addition, people began to notice his slurred speech and the stiffness of his movements.[96]

Spinks

Despite his apparent physical changes, Ali signed to fight his fifty-ninth professional fight against a young marine named Leon Spinks. Spinks, a light heavyweight gold medalist in the 1976 Montreal Olympics, had fought just seven professional fights. No one really expected Spinks to give Ali much trouble, least of all the champ himself, who trained lightly for the fight.

In their February 15, 1978, meeting, just a few weeks after Ali's thirty-sixth birthday, Leon Spinks came out at the be-

Leon Spinks is raised in victory after stripping Ali of his title in a fifteen-round bout.

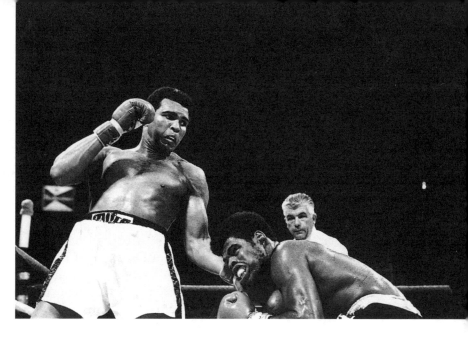

Ali delivers revenge on an out-of-shape Spinks during their rematch, becoming the only boxer in history to win the heavyweight crown three times.

ginning of the fight with the determination of a young bull. He administered a fierce, relentless beating to Ali. After fifteen rounds, Leon Spinks walked away as the new heavyweight champion.

Ali was philosophical. He knew he had not trained hard. He knew he was getting older. He knew, too, that Spinks was a tough fighter, and he gave Spinks credit for that. But Ali also knew that he had to get the title back. He could not retire now, after having been beaten. That was no way for his career to end. He demanded a rematch, and it was quickly granted.

By the time of their rematch on September 15, 1978, the roles had reversed. Now it was Ali in tip-top shape, eager and aggressive, presenting a painful boxing lesson to Spinks, who looked lethargic and out of shape. Spinks *was* out of shape. He had forsaken training and had spent the months before the rematch gambling, drinking, running with a wild crowd, and getting arrested for drug possession. The fight was one-sided, and when it was over Muhammad Ali was the only heavyweight boxer in history to have won the heavyweight crown three times.

Showing good sense, he announced his retirement on June 26, 1979, nine months after his triumph over Leon Spinks.

The Impossible Comeback

He now had time to do anything he wanted. He had time to spend with Veronica, their daughter Hana, and their second daughter, Laila. Ali also spent time visiting his children from his marriage to Belinda, although Belinda lived in Chicago and Muhammad and Veronica now lived in a mansion in Los Angeles. Ali had time to be in a movie called *Freedom Road* with Kris Kristofferson, and he spent a lot of time socializing with the Hollywood crowd.

In the meantime, with the heavyweight champ retired, a tournament was held to find a new champ, and Larry Holmes emerged triumphant. Holmes had superlative boxing skills and would dominate the

No Playing God

Ali's trainer Angelo Dundee saw the physical changes in Ali over the boxer's last few years in the ring. In Dave Anderson's book In the Corner, *Dundee explains that Ali was aware of what was happening all the time and capable of making his own decisions about continuing in this career:*

"Looking back, it's easy to say, but if I could pick when Muhammad should have stopped fighting, it would be after Manila. That was such a tough fight. We'd always had conversations about when he should stop. Back when he was a kid in the Fifth Street Gym in Miami, we had a pet joke about an old-time fighter who was skipping rope but his rhythm wasn't fluid. I'd say, 'See that guy over there, if you get like that I'm going to tell you, because he's stuttering.' Years later we'd be riding in a car somewhere and I'd lean back and say, 'Muhammad, you're starting to stutter.' He'd say, 'Oh, yeah. Oh, yeah.' He knew what I was saying. But he didn't want to stop. When Ferdie Pacheco [Ali's ring physician] started talking about how Muhammad should stop fighting, I resented it. I don't see anybody playing God in that situation. Muhammad did what he wanted to do."

heavyweight division for years. He had a lightning-fast jab that could knock a man out, and a canny ring sense. Once Ali's sparring partner, Holmes had always respected and admired the older man.

Ali, at age thirty-eight, could not stay out of the spotlight. Against the overwhelming advice of friends, family, and business advisors, the retired champ signed a contract to fight for the championship an unprecedented fourth time.

A master of persuasion, Ali had once convinced the world of his greatness. Now he still managed to convince some boxing authorities, such as Howard Cosell, that he could beat Holmes. As Ferdie Pacheco recalled, students of boxing were torn between what they wanted to see and what they knew would probably happen: "Everyone hoped, everyone prayed, but almost no one *believed.*"[97]

The few who believed were in for a disappointment. Ali was no match for Holmes in the November 1980 meeting. In fact, the match was an embarrassment for everyone in attendance, including Holmes and Ali. It was clear early in the bout that Ali had no strength, movement, or endurance, and soon Holmes, who had once been an employee of the Ali camp, began pulling his punches so as not to hurt his former boss. As the fight moved into the middle rounds, fans and media alike cried out for the referee to stop the fight, and even Holmes looked at the referee quizzically now and again, expressing his disgust with the beating he was administering. But each time the referee seemed to be considering stopping the fight, the winded Ali showed signs of rallying, and so the fight continued. Finally, in the eleventh round, Herbert Muhammad threw in the towel, ending the painful display.

Actor Sylvester Stallone, who had created his highly successful Rocky character after watching Chuck Wepner's heroic fight against Muhammad Ali years before, remembered the difficulty of watching the Holmes-Ali fight:

> Oh God, that was painful; like seeing your child playing on the railroad tracks with a train coming, and you can't get him out of the way. I just sat there and watched. It was like an autopsy on a man who's still alive. And I also felt for Larry Holmes, because he had a terrible job to do and he knew it. He had to go out and dismember a monument.[98]

Ali fought once more, against Trevor Berbick in Jamaica in 1981. Jamaica was chosen because Ali's management could not get any state to sanction an Ali fight.

Though he put up a decent fight, Ali lost the match in ten rounds, and his career was over—this time for good.

Now his medical problems, begun several years before, got worse. Author John Hennessey records the sadness surrounding Ali's exit from the boxing world:

> When he hung up his gloves forever late in 1981 his health was in shreds. Ali, the ultimate warrior, the wisecracking genius who always seemed smart enough to crack the brutal system which had bled champions dry since men first squared up to each other to provide sport, had succumbed to his pride for too long. Who could possibly have foreseen such a tragic ending to the most dazzling career of all?[99]

Parkinson's Syndrome

As far back as 1977 people close to Ali knew there was something wrong with the

Promoter Don King intercedes as Ali and Larry Holmes publicize their upcoming fight. The fight would turn out to be a painful embarassment for Ali.

Ali greets reporters with Reverend Jesse Jackson during the boxer's hospital stay. The years of sustaining repeated blows to the head had finally taken their toll: In 1984 Ali was diagnosed with Parkinson's syndrome.

champ's health. After his final fight in 1981 Ali's physical problems had become obvious. He spoke less and less, and when he did speak, his speech was slurred. He often seemed to have a faraway look in his eyes. He appeared to be slowing down physically, and he walked rigidly, like an older person with numerous aches and pains. People feared that he had suffered brain damage—and they were right. In 1984 Ali was diagnosed with Parkinson's syndrome.

Parkinson's syndrome is not the same as Parkinson's disease, which many people thought Ali might have had. Parkinson's disease is caused, in part, by genetic fac-

tors; that is, a person is at greater risk of getting it if someone in the family history has had it. Also, Parkinson's disease is a degenerative disease that gradually destroys the nervous system until serious and complete damage is done.

Parkinson's syndrome, which Ali has, does not necessarily have its origin in genetics. Rather, it can be caused by blows inflicted to the head, and this is the case for Ali. Also, Parkinson's syndrome means, in Ali's case, that the damage he incurred has stabilized—stopped—and probably will not get any worse.

What is Parkinson's syndrome? Basically, there is a problem between the connections of nerve and muscle. For instance, the brain gives an order to the mouth to say something, but because of damage to their connection, it takes a long time for the words to come out. This does not mean that the person with Parkinson's syndrome has lost intelligence. The same thought processes are going on, but it takes longer to express them. All of Ali's wit, humor, and sharpness of mind are there. It just takes longer for his words to come out after his brain gives the order.

The patient with Parkinson's syndrome has specific symptoms. Rigidity of the facial muscles—a condition known as the facial mask—is one of the most obvious signs. Slurred speech and general slowness of movement also indicate the presence of the syndrome. Ali has shown these effects.

The media and public response to Ali's condition has been strong. Tapes put together by groups and individuals opposed to boxing show young Cassius Clay bantering in front of the media and verbally harassing Sonny Liston. Then they show the retired Ali, slurring his speech, looking disinterested and distant. Citing cases of serious injury, such as that suffered by Ali, those people opposed to boxing insist it is a cruel and dangerous exhibition, serving no constructive purpose in society.

Writer Joyce Carol Oates, in her book of essays titled *On Boxing*, talks about the brutality of the sport:

> Boxing is the only sport in which the objective is to cause injury: the brain is the target, the knockout the goal. In one study it was estimated that 87 percent of boxers suffer some degree of

When comparing early photos of the brash, boastful Cassius Clay (left) with those of the retired Ali (right), the impact of Parkinson's is striking. Despite his symptoms—rigidity of facial muscles, slurred speech, and slowness of movement—Ali still has the same wit, humor, and sharpness of mind that he has always had.

Ali, who was always willing to accept the risks that went along with a boxing career, once stated, "I don't want anyone to feel sorry for me. . . . It would be bad if I had a disease that was contagious. Then I couldn't play with children and hug people all over the world."

brain damage in their lifetimes, no matter the relative success of their careers. And there is serious risk of eye injury as well.[100]

On the other hand, those who defend boxing argue that it has always been and remains a way out of poverty. Also, it is considered a manly art, a way to build character in young people. Finally, like race car drivers and cigarette smokers, the participants freely engage in the activity with full knowledge of the potential harm that may come.

Ali knew all along the physical risks that came along with a boxing career, and he never wanted anyone to pity him for the damage he suffered. Typically, in his retirement, he would see his own difficulties as a challenge and, moreover, a chance to test himself through his religious beliefs:

I don't want anyone to feel sorry for me. . . . It would be bad if I had a disease that was contagious. Then I couldn't play with children and hug people all over the world. But my problem with speaking bothers other people more than it bothers me. It doesn't stop me from doing what I want to do and being what I want to be. Sometimes I think that too many people put me on a pedestal before and made me into an idol. And that's against Islam; there are no idols in Islam. So maybe this problem I have is God's way of reminding me and everyone else about what's important. I accept it as God's will. And I know that God never gives anyone a burden that's too heavy for them to carry.[101]

A New Life

In the summer of 1986, after divorcing Veronica, Ali married his fourth wife, Yolanda Williams, also known as Lonnie. A devout Muslim, she had also grown up in Louisville, and her mother had been friends with Ali's mother. Lonnie provides Ali with a stable home life and support for his difficulties with Parkinson's syndrome.

He lives quietly now, on a farm in Michigan. He rises early in the morning,

In 1986 Ali married Yolanda Williams, a devout Muslim.

before sunrise, to perform the first of five daily prayers required of devout Muslims. Many days he lounges about the house, answering mail, signing his name on religious tracts he will distribute during his travels, and reviewing business matters with Lonnie, who holds a master of business administration degree. He likes visitors and often indulges them by putting on a videotape of one of his fights.

Ali gives his time to public appearances and charity events in the United States and abroad. For a special event he might donate some of his personal memorabilia. During the summer of 1993 he autographed headgear he had worn while in training and gave it away to be auctioned off. The proceeds went toward hospital costs for a boxer recently injured in a bout. Ali likes to work with children, and he enjoys surprising them with the magic tricks he has learned over the years.

The pace of life has slowed considerably for Muhammad Ali. Once he paraded through city streets, shouting his own name, swearing he would never be beaten, joyous fans following in his wake. Now he walks hesitantly because of his disease and is enveloped by those who recognize him, who are eager to see and hear him and shake the hand that knocked out Sonny Liston. Once he was the guest of heads of state

Ali, donning a robe that he donated to New York's Hard Rock Cafe, gets a hug from his daughter.

As a boxer he was, indeed, arguably the Greatest. In his early years as champion, he was described by writer Hugh McIlvanney as "a magnificently gifted and graceful boxer, the most aesthetically [artistically] satisfying the heavyweight division has known."[103] Further, he had a tremendous influence on the technical aspects of boxing, as Ronald Levao, in his essay "Reading the Fights," insists:

> He became Ali by creating the Ali style. It is a style for which there are antecedents [examples] in Jimmy Slattery, Gene Tunney, Kid Gavilan, and others, but one which he fashioned into so distinct a form that one might say of the way he turned his head or

To many fans all over the world, Muhammad Ali will always be "the Greatest."

in all corners of the globe, meeting important people, staying up all night. Now he relaxes contentedly at the end of the day, absorbed in the peace and serenity of the rolling countryside. He says his final prayer to Mecca at 11 P.M. before going to sleep.

Muhammad Ali is content. He says his life is really just beginning, that his boxing career and all that it encompassed was merely a prelude to his real reason for being on earth: "Fighting injustice, fighting racism, fighting crime, fighting illiteracy, fighting poverty, using this face the world knows so well, and going out and fighting for truth and different causes."[102]

Boxing was the perfect platform for Muhammad Ali. It demanded individualism, pitting one combatant against another in a battle of personal power, determination, and style—and Ali the boxer was a magnificent individualist, a stylist all his own.

Boxing Won't Be the Same

In 1967, just before being stripped of his championship, Ali spoke with author Robert Lipsyte. This excerpt is from Lipsyte's New York Times Magazine *article.*

"When I'm gone, boxing be nothing again. The fans with the cigars and the hats turned down'll be there, but not more housewives and little men on the street and foreign presidents. It's goin' to [go] back to the fighter who comes to town, smells a flower, visits a hospital, blows a horn and says he's in shape. Old hat. I was the onliest boxer in history people asked questions like a Senator."

countered over a jab what Coleridge said after reading the verses of a friend: "Had I met these lines running wild in the deserts of Arabia, I should have instantly screamed out 'Wordsworth!'" Ali's nuances and eccentricities provoked a world of observers to thunderous chants of recognition: "Ah-Lee! Ah-Lee!"[104]

Ali's wit and brashness were refreshing. Before Ali, boxers were asked how they felt and what they thought of their opponents, and their answers were predictable. Ali, though, bragged, insulted, made faces, and recited poetry. He mocked his opponents, scolded reporters, proclaimed his greatness. With the youthful Ali around, people knew something unpredictable would happen. Many first objected to his sense of showmanship; in time, people learned to look forward to it.

Behind his facade of youthful clowning Muhammad Ali was determinedly his own man. People saw that he would do what he wanted to do and what he felt was right, despite what prevailing, or common, moods or opinions flew in his face. He became a member of the Nation of Islam, thereby alienating African-American Christians who had supported him through his early career. Much to the concern of liberal blacks and whites who had applauded him for defeating the thuggish Sonny Liston, with his underworld connections, he spoke in favor of segregation and the second-class status of women. Later, he alienated radical blacks who objected to his declaration of support for Elijah Muhammad over the rebel, Malcolm X.

Before Ali, no individual in so prominent a position in American society and with so much to lose spoke out against the establishment for his political and religious beliefs. When Muhammad Ali took a stand against the Vietnam War by refusing induction, he in fact did lose everything he had worked his entire life for. He was stripped of his boxing title, refused the opportunity to earn his livelihood, and condemned to live offstage, in obscurity, by the forces of white America.

His courageous stand gave others the strength to stand up for their beliefs.

Americans—at first, younger Americans, but later most Americans—took heart from his opposition to the war in Vietnam and to all other unjust wars.

Ali's Importance to Blacks

Before Ali, no prominent black figures in America had successfully broken with the white establishment and flourished. Champion boxer Jack Johnson, who had flaunted his relationships with white women, had been hounded by authorities and finally arrested and thrown in jail on trumped-up charges. Lawyer, actor, and activist Paul Robeson was effectively exiled from America for criticizing its inability to provide dignity to its black population. Malcolm X was assassinated.

Ali, though, had survived and won. He joined the Nation of Islam and demanded to be called by his Muslim name, and he won. He wanted to change his management from the Louisville Sponsoring Group to Herbert Muhammad, and he won. Here was a black man who spurned the white world—its religion, its acquisitiveness, its wars—and insisted that God, Allah, was his only judge. How daring! He had spurned the establishment, refusing to play by its rules; he had declared himself free to be himself. He demanded—loudly, forcefully, wholeheartedly—to be free. And he won.

With Ali at the forefront, African Americans were reassured about the positive experience of being black. Baseball Hall of Famer Reggie Jackson puts it this way:

> Think about it! Do you understand what it did for black Americans to know that the most physically gifted,

possibly the most handsome, and one of the most charismatic [magnetically charming] men in the world was black? Ali helped raise black people in this country out of mental slavery. The entire experience of being black changed for millions of people because of Ali.[105]

In his retirement Muhammad Ali continues to be a positive force on people's lives. He responds to the difficulties of others as he always has—with compassion and generosity. A few years ago he saw on television that a New York home for the handicapped Jewish elderly was about to be closed for lack of funds. He immediately wrote out a check for one hundred thousand dollars, had it delivered, and asked that his identity not be disclosed.

Many blacks have been inspired by Ali, who loudly, forcefully, and wholeheartedly declared himself free to be himself, and won!

Ali, Sen. Daniel K. Inouye and former baseball great Joe DiMaggio (left) are awarded Ellis Island Medals of Honor in a tribute to America's ethnic diversity. Ali continues to be a positive role model for others.

Nonetheless, the story reached the media, and Ali refused to accept acclaim for his action. Robert Lipsyte reports that Ali could only express his bewilderment and anger over the idea that the home had nearly been closed:

> These poor crippled people came to this place to eat and talk with each other and draw a little and color, and that kept them alive. And no one else came up with the money. Didn't matter they were white or Jewish. Somebody's got to make a stand. Ain't nobody helping nobody in this country. It's dog eat dog. The dollar, the dollar, that's all they worry about.[106]

More Precious than Gold

Muhammad Ali has never worried about the dollar. His concern has always been with the things money could not buy. He discovered early that what the world considered precious—such as a gold Olympic medal—was not precious to him. He always wanted his life to stand for something else. And it has. Author Thomas Hauser writes:

> Ali stood for the propositions that principles mattered; that equality among people was just and proper; that all good things were possible. . . . Over time, the young man with a mischievous smile and sparkling eyes who entered our psyche [soul] at the 1960 Rome Olympics became the most famous person on earth. The world didn't just see or hear Ali. It felt him, and ultimately it fell in love with him.[107]

The world is still in love with him. He has become more than Muhammad Ali the great boxer, or Muhammad Ali the conscience of the sixties. He has become, quite simply, Muhammad Ali.

Notes

Introduction: The Forsaken Medal

1. Edna Rust and Art Rust Jr., *Art Rust's Illustrated History of the Black Athlete.* New York: Doubleday, 1985.
2. Rust, *Illustrated History of the Black Athlete.*
3. Rust, *Illustrated History of the Black Athlete.*
4. Muhammad Ali, with Richard Durham, *The Greatest: My Own Story.* New York: Random House, 1975.

Chapter 1: Cassius Clay

5. Ferdie Pacheco, *Muhammad Ali: A View from the Corner.* New York: Carol Publishing, 1992.
6. Huston Horn, "Who Made Me—Is Me!" *Sports Illustrated,* September 25, 1969.
7. Horn, "Who Made Me—Is Me!"
8. Thomas Hauser, *Muhammad Ali: His Life and Times.* New York: Simon and Schuster, 1991.
9. Horn, "Who Made Me—Is Me!"
10. Rust, *Illustrated History of the Black Athlete.*
11. Horn, "Who Made Me—Is Me!"
12. Hauser, *Muhammad Ali: His Life and Times.*
13. Ali, with Durham, *The Greatest.*
14. Thomas Conklin, *Muhammad Ali: The Fight for Respect.* Brookfield, CT: New Directions, The Millbrook Press, 1991.
15. Ali, with Durham, *The Greatest.*
16. Audrey Edwards, with Gary Wohl, *Muhammad Ali: The People's Champ.* Boston: Little, Brown, 1977.
17. Arthur Daly, "Man with a Future," *New York Times,* May 14, 1961.
18. Horn, "Who Made Me—Is Me!"
19. Horn, "Who Made Me—Is Me!"
20. Daly, "Man with a Future."

Chapter 2: "Who Made Me—Is Me!"

21. Robert Lipsyte, *Free to Be Muhammad Ali.* New York: Harper and Row, 1978.
22. Dave Anderson, *In the Corner.* New York: William Morrow, 1991.
23. Horn, "Who Made Me—Is Me!"
24. Horn, "Who Made Me—Is Me!"
25. Anderson, *In the Corner.*
26. Hauser, *Muhammad Ali: His Life and Times.*
27. Daly, "Man with a Future."
28. John Hennessey, *Muhammad Ali: "The Greatest."* New York: Smithmark, 1991.
29. "Clear Up the Liston Case," *Sports Illustrated,* August 29, 1960.
30. Huston Horn, "A Rueful Dream Come True," *Sports Illustrated,* November 18, 1963.
31. Gilbert Rogin, "Campaign's End for an Ancient Warrior," *Sports Illustrated,* November 26, 1962.
32. Pacheco, *Muhammad Ali: A View from the Corner.*
33. Pacheco, *Muhammad Ali: A View from the Corner.*
34. Ali, with Durham, *The Greatest.*

Chapter 3: A New Champion for a New Decade

35. Huston Horn, "The First Days in the New Life of the Champion of the World," *Sports Illustrated,* March 9, 1964.
36. Robert H. Boyle, "This Is What Clay Says He Wants," *Sports Illustrated,* August 5, 1963.
37. Robert H. Boyle, "Sonny Slams Ahead," *Sports Illustrated,* July 29, 1963.
38. Boyle, "This Is What Clay Says He Wants."
39. Norman Mailer, "King of the World," in Joyce Carol Oates and Daniel Halpern, eds., *Reading the Fights.* New York: Henry Holt, 1988.

40. Boyle, "This Is What Clay Says He Wants."

41. Cassius Clay, "I'm a Little Special," *Sports Illustrated*, February 24, 1964.

42. Anderson, *In the Corner*.

43. Pacheco, *Muhammad Ali: A View from the Corner*.

44. Tex Maule, "Yes, It Was Good and Honest," *Sports Illustrated*, March 9, 1964.

45. Mailer, "King of the World," in Oates and Halpern, eds., *Reading the Fights*.

46. Hauser, *Muhammad Ali: His Life and Times*.

47. Horn, "The First Days in the New Life of the Champion of the World."

48. Horn, "The First Days in the New Life of the Champion of the World."

49. Ali, with Durham, *The Greatest*.

50. Anderson, *In the Corner*.

51. Robert Lipsyte, "I'm Free to Be Who I Want," *New York Times Magazine*, May 28, 1967.

52. Conklin, *Muhammad Ali: The Fight for Respect*.

Chapter 4: "Ain't Got No Quarrel"

53. Conklin, *Muhammad Ali: The Fight for Respect*.

54. Conklin, *Muhammad Ali: The Fight for Respect*.

55. Arthur Daly, "Is This Trip Necessary?" *New York Times*, March 29, 1966.

56. Jeffrey T. Sammons, *Beyond the Ring: The Role of Boxing in American Society*. Chicago: University of Illinois Press, 1990.

57. Neil Laufer and Thomas Hauser, *Muhammad Ali: Memories*. New York: Rizzoli International, 1992.

58. Ali, with Durham, *The Greatest*.

59. Ali, with Durham, *The Greatest*.

60. Gerald Eskenazi, "Chuvalo Talks Tough as Clay Makes Jokes," *New York Times*, March 28, 1966.

61. Lipsyte, *Free to Be Muhammad Ali*.

62. Lipsyte, *Free to Be Muhammad Ali*.

63. Robert H. Boyle, "Champ in the Jug?" *Sports Illustrated*, April 10, 1967.

64. Boyle, "Champ in the Jug?"

65. Howard Cosell, in Hauser, *Muhammad Ali: His Life and Times*.

66. Ali, with Durham, *The Greatest*.

67. Bill Russell, with Tex Maule, "I Am Not Worried About Ali," *Sports Illustrated*, June 19, 1967.

Chapter 5: Exile and Return

68. Daniel Preston, *Twentieth Century United States History*. New York: HarperCollins, 1992.

69. Hauser, *Muhammad Ali: His Life and Times*.

70. Pacheco, *Muhammad Ali: A View from the Corner*.

71. Ali, with Durham, *The Greatest*.

72. Ali, with Durham, *The Greatest*.

73. Hugh McIlvanney, "Superman at Bay," in Oates and Halpern, eds., *Reading the Fights*.

74. Ali, with Durham, *The Greatest*.

75. Anderson, *In the Corner*.

76. Bryant Gumbel, in Hauser, *Muhammad Ali: His Life and Times*.

77. Lipsyte, *Free to Be Muhammad Ali*.

78. McIlvanney, "Superman at Bay," in Oates and Halpern, eds., *Reading the Fights*.

Chapter 6: Winning Back the Title

79. Anderson, *In the Corner*.

80. Anderson, *In the Corner*.

81. Pacheco, *Muhammad Ali: A View from the Corner*.

82. Ali, with Durham, *The Greatest*.

83. Ali, with Durham, *The Greatest*.

84. Ali, with Durham, *The Greatest*.

85. Ali, with Durham, *The Greatest*.

86. Lipsyte, *Free to Be Muhammad Ali*.

87. Ali, with Durham, *The Greatest*.

88. Ali, with Durham, *The Greatest*.

Chapter 7: Too Long in the Ring

89. Hauser, *Muhammad Ali: His Life and Times.*

90. Mark Kram, "Manila for Blood and for Money," *Sports Illustrated*, September 29, 1975.

91. Hennessey, *Muhammad Ali: "The Greatest."*

92. Laufer and Hauser, *Muhammad Ali: Memories.*

93. Pacheco, *Muhammad Ali: A View from the Corner.*

94. Pacheco, *Muhammad Ali: A View from the Corner.*

95. Ferdie Pacheco, in Hauser, *Muhammad Ali: His Life and Times.*

96. Pacheco, *Muhammad Ali: A View from the Corner.*

97. Pacheco, *Muhammad Ali: A View from the Corner.*

98. Laufer and Hauser, *Muhammad Ali: Memories.*

99. Hennessey, *Muhammad Ali: "The Greatest."*

100. Joyce Carol Oates, *On Boxing.* New York: Dolphin/Doubleday, 1987.

101. Conklin, *Muhammad Ali: The Fight for Respect.*

Epilogue: A New Life

102. Hauser, *Muhammad Ali: His Life and Times.*

103. McIlvanney, "Superman at Bay," in Oates and Halpern, eds., *Reading the Fights.*

104. Ronald Levao, "Reading the Fights," in Oates and Halpern, eds., *Reading the Fights.*

105. Laufer and Hauser, *Muhammad Ali: Memories.*

106. Lipsyte, *Free to Be Muhammad Ali.*

107. Laufer and Hauser, *Muhammad Ali: Memories.*

For Further Reading

Muhammad Ali, with Richard Durham, *The Greatest: My Own Story*. New York: Random House, 1975. Part truth, part tall tale, Ali's autobiography is completely entertaining. This work is valuable for the recording of Ali's feelings about a number of events, including his involvement with the Nation of Islam, his refusal to accept induction into the armed forces, and some of his more celebrated bouts. No photographs.

Dave Anderson, *In the Corner*. New York: William Morrow, 1991. Regarded as one of the best insider books on boxing, this work is a compilation of accounts through the eyes of boxing's noted trainers, including Angelo Dundee, Eddie Futch, and Lou Duva. Revealing and amusing anecdotes abound, and several stunning black-and-white photographs are included.

Thomas Hauser, *Muhammad Ali: His Life and Times*. New York: Simon and Schuster, 1991. The best book written yet on the life of Muhammad Ali. The author makes use of the witness technique, whereby the feelings, opinions, and anecdotes of those contemporary with Muhammad Ali—Sylvester Stallone, Jimmy Carter, and Bob Dylan, among many others—form the skeleton of the book. Fine black-and-white photos grace this definitive biography, which was also a national bestseller.

Neil Laufer and Thomas Hauser, *Muhammad Ali: Memories*. New York: Rizzoli International, 1992. Superlative color images by Laufer, a photographer who followed Ali throughout his career, and moving, complimentary text by Hauser make this coffee-table-sized volume a fine place to begin for those interested in the life and times of the Greatest.

Robert Lipsyte, *Free to Be Muhammad Ali*. New York: Harper and Row, 1978. One of the first biographies of Muhammad Ali, and one of the best. Journalist Lipsyte provides an easy-to-read, fast-moving account of Ali, valuable for the author's wit and his willingness to expose various myths that grew up around the fighter.

Joyce Carol Oates and Daniel Halpern, eds., *Reading the Fights*. New York: Henry Holt, 1988. The editors have put together an impressive sampling of essays dealing with the world of boxing, written by such acknowledged masters of the form as A.J. Liebling, Norman Mailer, and George Plimpton. This book is valuable for its varying viewpoints and writing styles and for its two essays concerning Ali, by writers Mailer and Hugh McIlvanney. No photographs.

Ferdie Pacheco, *Muhammad Ali: A View from the Corner*. New York: Carol Publishing, 1992. One of the more intimate books about Muhammad Ali, written by the official physician of the Ali camp. Pacheco's account includes chapters titled "The Ali Circus," which discusses Ali's entourage, or followers, and "Ali and the Ladies." Pacheco also provides a complete and simple explanation of Parkinson's syndrome and its effects on Muhammad Ali, and finally, a complete ring record detailing Ali's professional career.

Additional Works Consulted

Books

Thomas Conklin, *Muhammad Ali: The Fight for Respect*. Brookfield, CT: New Directions, The Millbrook Press, 1991. Award-winning writer Thomas Conklin puts the Muhammad Ali story within the context of a society challenged from within by racial tensions and the Vietnam War.

Audrey Edwards, with Gary Wohl, *Muhammad Ali: The People's Champ*. Boston: Little, Brown, 1977. A fine overview of the boxer's life up until his victory over George Foreman. Good selection of black-and-white photographs.

Thomas Hauser, *The Black Lights: Inside the World of Professional Boxing*. New York: McGraw-Hill, 1986. Thomas Hauser's true account of three months in the life of professional boxing champion Billy Costello paints a graphic, inside picture of the world of professional boxing.

John Hennessey, *Muhammad Ali: "The Greatest."* New York: Smithmark, 1991. Fine color photographs and perceptive commentary grace this oversized volume, making it a welcome addition to the Ali fan's collection.

Joyce Carol Oates, *On Boxing*. New York: Dolphin/Doubleday, 1987. Written by one of America's finest writers, this small volume provides a wonderfully varied and literate look at the boxing world and includes many stunning black-and-white photographs.

Daniel Preston, *Twentieth Century United States History*. New York: Harper-Collins, 1992. Daniel Preston has written a clear, well-organized text that outlines and discusses America and its role in this century's major events, including the Vietnam War.

Edna Rust and Art Rust Jr., *Art Rust's Illustrated History of the Black Athlete*. New York: Doubleday, 1985. This well-written, oversized volume contains a formidable amount of information about black athletes and leaves the reader impressed with their important contributions to the world of sports.

Jeffrey T. Sammons, *Beyond the Ring: The Role of Boxing in American Society*. Chicago: University of Illinois Press, 1990. Jeffrey Sammons's provocative work explores the history of the relationship between American values and boxing and illuminates the significance of boxing greats, including Joe Louis and Muhammad Ali.

Jose Torres, *Sting Like a Bee: The Muhammad Ali Story*. New York: Abelard-Schuman, 1971. Former light heavyweight boxing champion of the world Jose Torres has combined accounts of his own ringside responses to three Ali fights with a straightforward biography of Ali in this essential work, which also includes a preface by American writer Norman Mailer.

Periodicals

Robert H. Boyle, "Champ in the Jug?" *Sports Illustrated*, April 10, 1967.

Robert H. Boyle, "Sonny Slams Ahead," *Sports Illustrated*, July 29, 1963.

Robert H. Boyle, "This Is What Clay Says He Wants," *Sports Illustrated*, August 5, 1963.

Cassius Clay, "I'm a Little Special," *Sports Illustrated*, February 24, 1964.

"Clear Up the Liston Case," *Sports Illustrated*, August 29, 1960.

Arthur Daly, "Is This Trip Necessary?" *New York Times*, March 29, 1966.

Arthur Daly, "Man with a Future," *New York Times*, May 14, 1961.

Angelo Dundee, with Tex Maule, "He Could Go to Jail and Still Be Champ," *Sports Illustrated*, August 28, 1967.

Gerald Eskenazi, "Chuvalo Talks Tough as Clay Makes Jokes," *New York Times*, March 28, 1966.

Huston Horn, "The First Days in the New Life of the Champion of the World," *Sports Illustrated*, March 9, 1964.

Huston Horn, "A Rueful Dream Come True," *Sports Illustrated*, November 18, 1963.

Huston Horn, "Who Made Me—Is Me!" *Sports Illustrated*, September 25, 1969.

Mark Kram, "Manila for Blood and for Money," *Sports Illustrated*, September 29, 1975.

Robert Lipsyte, "I'm Free to Be Who I Want," *New York Times Magazine*, May 28, 1967.

Tex Maule, "Yes, It Was Good and Honest," *Sports Illustrated*, March 9, 1964.

Gilbert Rogin, "Campaign's End for an Ancient Warrior," *Sports Illustrated*, November 26, 1962.

Bill Russell, with Tex Maule, "I Am Not Worried About Ali," *Sports Illustrated*, June 19, 1967.

Index

Picture Credits

Cover photo by UPI/Bettmann

AP/Wide World Photos, 10, 12, 13, 15, 19 (top), 20, 21, 22, 23, 24, 25, 27, 29 (top), 30, 31, 32, 33, 36, 40, 41, 42, 44, 46, 53, 54, 56, 57, 58, 59, 61 (both), 63, 67 (bottom), 69 (bottom), 74, 76, 77, 79, 83, 85, 86 (top), 89, 91, 94, 95 (right), 96, 97, 98 (top), 100, 101

The Bettmann Archive, 11, 16 (top), 19 (bottom)

National Archives, 49

UPI/Bettmann, 7, 9, 16 (bottom), 17, 26, 29 (bottom), 35, 37, 38, 43, 45, 47, 50, 51, 52, 62, 64, 66, 67 (top), 69 (top), 71, 72, 73, 75, 80, 81, 82, 86 (bottom), 88, 90, 93, 95 (left), 98 (bottom)

About the Author

Arthur Diamond, born in Queens, New York, received a bachelor's degree in English from the University of Oregon and a master's degree in English/Writing from Queens College.

Mr. Diamond is the author of several nonfiction books, including *The Bhopal Chemical Leak* and *Smallpox and the American Indian* in Lucent Books' World Disasters series, as well as Lucent Books' *The Importance of Jackie Robinson* and *The Importance* of *Anwar Sadat*. He lives in New York with wife Irina and their children, Benjamin Thomas and Jessica Ann.